ANDROID DEVELOPMENT FOR GIFTED PRIMATES

Antonis Tsagaris

Dedication

I dedicate this book to pizza.

That's right: pizza. Pizza gave me sustenance when I was weak, strength when I had almost lost hope.

Also my son. Who is almost as cool as pizza.

Did I just write that?

Let's hope there's never a custody battle.

Reviews Matter

If you enjoy this book, please consider leaving a review at Amazon at https://www.amazon.com/Android-Development-Gifted-Primates-Beginners-ebook/dp/B07FYSKVYY/

This is my first book and it needs all the help it can get!

Contents

ANDROID DEVELOPMENT FOR GIFTED PRIMATES — 1

Dedication — 2

Reviews Matter — 3

Contents — 4

About the author & the book — 9

Prerequisites — 14

Should I learn Java before starting Android development? — 14

A new contender has emerged: Kotlin — 16

Ok, I believe you. Show me the Java! — 18

I'm back! Armed with the basics of Java, I will conquer the Play Store — 22

Android Development Ultra-Basics — 24

What I wish I knew before starting Android development — 24

The four components of Android — 25

Activity — 25

Broadcast Receiver — 25

Service — 26

Content Provider — 26

The UI Thread — 27

Use libraries — 28

The Nitty-Gritty   **30**

AndroidManifest.xml   30

Usual Pitfalls, The Movie   31

build.gradle   32

XML: Layouts, Resources and Assets   **35**

The activity_main.xml file   36

Views and ViewGroups   37

Views   38

View   38

TextView   38

ImageView   39

EditText   39

A Note on creating user interfaces in Java   39

Adding and customizing Views   40

Adding Views   40

A Note on Dimension Measurements in Android   43

Customizing Views   46

The one attribute you'll be using all the time   46

TextView   47

ImageView   49

Oh, dang! These are a lot of scale types!   53

EditText   54

Common View attributes   56

ViewGroups   63

    LinearLayout   64

    RelativeLayout   72

    FrameLayout   81

    ScrollView   83

    A Note on Nesting   84

    AdapterViews   86

Resources and R.java   93

Accessing resources in XML   103

Accessing resources in Java code   108

    A Note on Method Overloading   113

Getting Java with it: Coding the app   **120**

The Activity   120

    Scenic Detour: Activities and Configuration Changes   123

    Interacting with elements in your Activity   129

    Scenic Detour: Running your app   134

    Getting some visible output   138

        First way: use the Android Monitor section in Android Studio 138

        Second way: change something in your UI (not recommended) 140

    Baby's (Second) First Program   143

    Launching another Activity and some info on the onBackPressed() method 154

Intents   156

     Parental Advisory! Explicit Intents!   156

     Implicit Intents   158

     Passing data between components using Intents   162

     FIRST AND ONLY SUMMARY YOU'LL EVER SEE IN THIS BOOK   166

     And another thing: startActivityForResult()   168

     SCENIC DETOUR: King Kong taking a dump   170

Shared Preferences: saving data locally like a boss   173

Services   190

     A Story from the Trenches   191

     Types of Services   192

     Stopping a Service   194

     In which thread does a Service run?   195

     IntentService   196

       So, no drawbacks?   197

       An example of an IntentService   197

Bonus awesome: NotificationManager, Notification and Notification.Builder   206

     Creating and showing notifications   206

     Accessing system services   207

Broadcast Receivers & You   213

     Radio Days: an analogy about Broadcast Receivers   214

     System events   217

Manifest-registered Broadcast Receivers 219

Context-registered Broadcast Receivers 222

.sendBroadcast() and your own radio station 226

Sending data between components 231

Broadcasting the data from the Intent Service 231

Receiving the data in the Activity 233

A final note **240**

About the author & the book

You don't know me. My name is Antonis Tsagaris and I'm the Android developer for codehouse five, maker/co-founder of such services as Karkoona, Looxie and (coming soon, or depending on when I finish this book, possibly 45 years ago) YourBook.

My apps have been featured in Android Police, Android Guys, Phandroid, PhoneArena, AndroidWorld.nl, InBusiness and VentureBeat, among others. Mom was wrong — it feels awesome to gloat!

I haven't always been an Android developer.

I was born in 1980 in the small town of Larnaca, Cyprus. If you haven't heard of Cyprus, don't be upset: it's a small, occasionally beautiful rock in the Mediterranean, sandwiched between Egypt and Turkey. And get this: a couple of our beaches are consistently included in Best 25 Beaches In Europe lists!

From an early age, I was a freaking nerd. I was also a pretty creative guy. Some of my projects included The Bones, a series of ten mini books (about 3 pages each) about someone rubbing a bone (I had no idea about double entendres yet, you sicko), which resulted in a miraculous resurrection of dinosaurs in a nearby salt lake from which only the *Spaceship Ex Machina* USS Enterprise could save us. I am not even kidding.

Another one was a video game programmed in QBasic in the MS-DOS 5 days. It was a hybrid text/graphic adventure called *Invaders Of The Lost Country*. Which was a misleading title, since it was the invaders themselves that were from the Lost Country, so it should have been *Invaders **From** The Lost Country, You Fucking Idiot*. I am still not over it. All of the source code was on a 80286 PC I owned at the time, which my mom (MOOOOOM!!) threw away , so I can't even make it right by retconning the shit of it.

Ooh, one more. I made a metagame in GW-Basic called *The Operator*. The objective of the game was getting out of it without resorting to using **ctrl+C.** One of the proudest achievements of my life was lulling my super-computer savvy and also coder cousin Tefkros (now a Karkoona co-founder and I'm his best man, so I guess he doesn't hold a grudge) into a false sense of accomplishment by having the program show him what seemed like a DOS command prompt. Guess what happened when he typed 'cls' to clear the screen? He got "fuck you" as an output. Oh yes. That was some Sixth Sense-level plot twist right there.

Strangely, my family and friends were doing nothing to dissuade this behaviour. My dad signed me up for Pascal classes. I was doing pretty well, until pointers were brought up. I'm still having nightmares about pointers.

My godmother got me a couple of walkie-talkies and made me promise that I'd break them apart and rip their guts out to find out how they worked when I was bored with them. They are still intact and she knows nothing about it.

Chemistry sets were my regular present every Christmas. I loved the colors of copper sulfate and phenolphthalein mixed with bases. Someone got me an electronic set, so I set up my own tiny radio station to broadcast in the neighborhood, until I realized that I had nothing to broadcast, other than farts. Even farts lose their luster once you've overdone them.

After deciding I loved biology, I got a degree in dentistry and later a MSc in oral surgery. I am still practising.

Having an oral surgeon teach you Android development may sound counterintuitive, but think about it: I've been developing Android apps for five years. During these five years, I've learned about and practiced a lot of stuff. What offers me a somewhat unique perspective (among people writing books about Android development, anyway) is the fact that I still haven't forgotten about all the things that first made me scratch and then bang my against the wall when I was first starting out.

Which means that this is not your run-of-the-mill book about Android development (not that there's anything wrong with those).

This book will guide you through taking your first steps with confidence, without having to wonder "what now?" the entire time, which is what I had to go through for the first year or so of my Android development self-training.

It follows that, by design, this book is highly opinionated. My answer to "should I learn Java before starting Android development?" is not "it depends", it is "you bet!".

You will learn about my journey. Hear about stories in the (literal) trenches. You will read a treatise about King Kong's digestive tract and his defecation habits (for real). You will have to trust an oral surgeon to teach you about the Android SDK. You will possibly laugh. You will almost certainly not cry.

And you'll definitely learn how to start an Intent Service.

The Basics

Prerequisiteş

Should I learn Java before starting Android development?

You bet!

Keep in mind that I am talking about native Android development here, not the cross-platform, web-container-as-app, "I fart in your general direction" way of insulting your audience. As you can tell, I feel pretty strongly about this — and why wouldn't I? Have you ever compared the experience of using a native, Java-made app with that of using a JavaScript/CSS/HTML5 abomination?

If you have, you know what I'm talking about. If you haven't, please go and download Google's own "Arts & Culture" app and tap on a photo of a painting. Then go in the Play Store app, do a search and click on a search result. You may notice that the icon of the search result in the Play Store glides smoothly into place in the next screen (this is something called a shared element transition, introduced in Lollipop) and you may also notice the photo of the painting in the Arts & Culture app crash and glitch into place in the next screen (this is called a spazznimation, introduced in non-native apps).

Maybe you don't care. If you don't, this book is not for you. Ask for a refund immediately.

If you do care, please understand that going the full native Android path has enormous benefits, including but not limited to faster loading times, smoother animations, consistent and reusable user interface elements that already look familiar to your prospective user and excellent, official tooling with the newest API level support. Also, you'll be more attractive to the opposite sex.

Not convinced yet? Want another reason to go for Java? Two words: Stack Overflow. Since Java is the language of choice for Android development, most of the development tends on happen using Java. Have a problem? Some stupid bug you can't quite make sense of? Chances are, Stack Overflow has you covered. Try doing the same thing if you're using phonegap or Xamarin or whatever. I dare you. You'll be lucky if you end up on a site about the dietary habits of the mountain gorilla.

A new contender has emerged: Kotlin

Now you might say "what about Kotlin? I heard that it's the new hotness and I like hotness".

Even though before starting to write this book I hadn't bothered with Kotlin a lot (I just read the occasional article about how awesome it was), I went ahead and took an online video course and read a book (https://leanpub.com/kotlin-for-android-developers) just so I know what I'm talking about. That's how much I care for you, dear reader.

Anyway. Kotlin has a lot of advantages that are difficult to deny: it's made by JetBrains so it integrates effortlessly with Android Studio and IntelliJ IDEA, it has great stuff like extension functions (my favorite part of it, actually), package-level variables, lambdas, default arguments, no **new** keyword everywhere, automatic conversion from Java to Kotlin (it's really impressive to see it in action) and, in addition to all that, it is so much less verbose than Java. Maybe you don't understand (some of) what I just said but most coders consider the above A Good Thing.

So, that seals it, then? I should just go ahead and use Kotlin, right?

Remember when I said that this is a highly opinionated book? Well, here's another opinion:

No.

At the risk of causing most Android developers to go for the pitchforks and invoking the wrath of Jake Wharton, I have to say that if you're just starting out, it would be wise to still go for Java.

While Kotlin is an *amazing* language, I would like you to think of Java's verbose syntax (which means having to write quite a lot of code, more than a lot of other languages) as an advantage at this point. Java makes you write everything, sometimes twice. There's not much "elegance" to be found in

```
NotAgain notAgain = new
NotAgain();
```

since you have to declare the type of the variable (NotAgain) twice and use the **new** keyword but it tells you the type of the variable with no inference involved, it lets you know that it creates a new instance of it and the semicolon is the cherry on top that says "anything following this character is a new statement".

Maybe after getting the hang of it, switch to Kotlin. But for now, my opinion is that you *need* a language that is essentially self-documenting and that has a huge amount of available help on StackOverflow. Not to mention that the official Android documentation is in Java.

Ok, I believe you. Show me the Java!

What? No! Java is a huge subject so you'll have to do that somewhere else.

"But wait. You have been preaching Java for at least a thousand words now. What do you suggest I do?"

Fair enough. I will share with you the most useful resources I have used myself to learn Java.

What I did at first was get a book called Java For Android Developers. I wanted something focused and more Android-oriented than a general Java book. After getting the book I started making notes but I couldn't even make it halfway through before despairing and thinking that this was an impossible task. It didn't help that the book was full-on technical and drier than the Sahara desert if the Sahara desert was on Mars.

I then did the unthinkable (for me) and decided to watch some video tutorials, even though at the time I was, for some inexplicable reason, highly suspicious of video tutorials. And that's when things started to click.

Watching John Purcell's "Java Tutorial For Complete Beginners" (which is available for free on Udemy https://www.udemy.com/java-tutorial/ and YouTube https://www.youtube.com/watch?v=7WiPGP_0AUA&list=PL9DF 6E4B45C36D411) was a huge turning point. John sounds like a saintly person and he is really patient with explaining some really challenging stuff. You'll learn a lot.

Team Treehouse (https://teamtreehouse.com/) requires a monthly subscription (which currently costs $25 USD) but has a huge library of Java and Android-specific tutorials that are labeled "Beginner", "Intermediate" and "Advanced". If you ask me, the subscription price is too low (and no, I'm not part of Team Treehouse or an affiliate, just a huge fan). Initially, you may be put off by the extremely whimsical atmosphere of the tutorials (I know I almost was —I mean, they have a frog mascot) but give them a chance.
Be advised, though: do not simply watch the tutorials. Pick up a notebook and a pen and **write down the code of the examples,** even if you don't fully understand it yet.
After you've written down the code, install the Java Development Kit (JDK, full instructions for your OS of choice on

the Oracle site), fire up your Java IDE (Integrated Development Environment) of choice (two very popular ones are Eclipse and IntelliJ IDEA, though I suggest the latter because of its extreme similarity to Android Studio—it is made by the same company after all) and then **type and execute the code.**

You **do not** need an *encyclopedic* knowledge of the language, you need a *working* knowledge of it. Simply watching the tutorials will make you *think* that you understand something but you'll be so far removed from its execution that you'll forget it within a day or two. Trust me on this, **you cannot skip it.**

Of course, with Java being a language with a huge standard library, you need to focus on some very specific stuff to make progress. When I was starting out, the CommonsWare book "The Busy Coder's Guide to Android Development" really helped me get going by suggesting a range of subjects I should focus on. I have trimmed that list down even further:

- **Language syntax, fundamentals and flow control**
- **Classes and objects**
- **The Java type system**
- **The Java Collections Framework and Generics**
- **Threads**
- **Methods**
- **Exceptions and try / catch blocks**
- **Interfaces**

- **Scoping**

Visit https://en.wikibooks.org/wiki/Java_Programming for a really good reference for the above. Don't forget to watch video tutorials.

ANTONIS TSAGARIS

I'm back! Armed with the basics of Java, I will conquer the Play Store

Erm... hate to break this to you but... have you heard of XML?

Yeah.

Here is the XML definition from Wikipedia:

> **Extensible Markup Language (XML)** *is a markup language that defines a set of rules for encoding documents in a format that is both human-readable and machine-readable.*

And it's true: XML is human-readable and the best way to create your user interface in Android. Other developers may disagree, since there is a graphical drag-and-drop editor (the Interface Builder) in Android Studio that you could use.

I don't care: XML is so easy to understand and apply (at least when designing user interfaces for Android apps) and gives you so much control that (Opinionated Book Warning) any attempt to exclusively use the graphical editor will always end in frustration. Sure, you can start using it to get going, place some buttons on the screen and feel amazing for a couple of hours

22

but I promise you that you'll return to XML if you want to get anything serious done.

The good news is that XML is a markup language, so it simply describes stuff: where your user interface items (called **views**) will be placed, how big they will be etc. so you won't have to go hunting for tutorials: I will show you what you need to know in this book as we progress.

Android Development Ultra-Basics

What I wish I knew before starting Android development

I have been developing for Android for 4 years, so I am in a very unique position: it hasn't been so long that I'm totally disconnected from the experience of a beginner but it has been long enough for me to gain the skills I need to create beautiful, functional apps.

In this book, I plan to share with you *my personal experience.* Things change a lot in retrospect and, as I've discovered during the past 4 years, those well-intentioned books that tried to teach me everything, while technically exhaustive, had me scratching my head quite a lot of the time.

So I'll be leaving some stuff out. This is stuff that I consider non-essential for a beginner and I wish I had someone to tell me "Antonis, don't bother with this" when it was just starting out.

With that said, let's get going.

The four components of Android

Activity

An activity represents a screen with a user interface. This may seem counterintuitive, since we associate the word "activity" with getting something done (eg. jogging or cooking) but get used to it. **An activity is a screen of your application.**

Broadcast Receiver

According to the Android API Guide, *a broadcast receiver is a component that responds to system-wide broadcast announcements.*

What does that mean? An announcement could be the system saying "hey, your device's battery is getting low" or "you have just lost network connection" so that your app can do something about it. This sort of announcement is not limited to the system: a third-party app could send a broadcast about an event and another app could intercept it and do something about it.

Service

A service runs in the background to perform some kind of long-running task. This could be downloading a file from the web, calculating a complex result or even playing a song in the background. There are two kinds of services, started and bound services. In this book, I'll mostly be talking about the sweetest kind of service, a subclass of the Service class called **IntentService**. It is not perfect for everything (what is?) but it is so convenient to use that it's what I usually use.

Content Provider

A content provider manages a shared set of app data. It's an abstraction that must implement a standard set of APIs (Application Programming Interface) so that different apps can use the same data.
I seriously wish I had someone tell me "Do not bother with Content Providers yet" in the early days. I cannot stress this enough. The API is quite convoluted for beginners and it's very rarely (if ever) that you'll need to create one. You may need to *access* one but again, it's better to learn about them when the time comes to use them. This book will not be containing any more info about Content Providers. Good riddance.

The UI Thread

The official Java documentation defines a Thread as a thread of execution in a program. That's... helpful, I guess? Anyway, you can have multiple threads running at the same time, each one performing its own thing independently of the others. Maybe one thread is performing some sort of network action while another one is playing back a song.

That's all fine and dandy but there's one thread that you shouldn't use to perform long-running operations and that's the UI (AKA main) thread.

Blocking the main UI thread is a Very Bad Idea™

If you perform long-running tasks on the UI thread, your application will become unresponsive (and good luck pressing any buttons or interacting with the device in any way when that happens). The user experience if going to suffer. It gets worse: if the main thread gets blocked for a long time, your application will crash (and burn) by throwing an Application Not Responding (ANR) error. Eek!

So, again, how do you avoid ANR errors? Simple: you don't run long-running tasks on the UI thread. One of the most usual types of long-running tasks is network communication, like downloading or uploading data. This should always be done on a thread other than the main one, because even if the amount of data you're transferring is tiny, you have no idea how fast (or slow) the connection is. A simple way to do this is use a networking library like Square's Retrofit or Picasso (for images) and let them take care of business. Which brings me into the other thing I wish I knew (and took to heart) at the start of my Android developer career, which is...

Use libraries

Coders are makers. People that like to look under the surface and see how things work. Understand what makes them tick (that sounded a bit serial-murdery). So I totally get you: you don't want to use a library to make things simple. You don't want to write a couple of lines using Retrofit and have that JSON data downloaded and automagically converted into objects for you.

Nope. You want to use `HttpUrlConnection`. You *have* to use `JSONObject` and `JSONArray`. Do it by yourself.

And, again, I totally get you: that's exactly how I was — but hear me out.

First of all, `HttpUrlConnection` and `JSONObject` were not created *ex nihilo*. Very talented developers sat down, wrote and (most importantly) *debugged the shit* out of them. You know why they did that? For other people to use so that they won't have to keep reinventing the wheel. So even if you use them instead of Retrofit, you're not "doing everything yourself", as you've undoubtedly led yourself into believing. You're still standing on the shoulders of giants but they are now slightly drunk and unstable (mostly because of you) giants.

Secondly, think about why you want to become an Android developer. It's to make things and be proud of them! Anything that can help you get there faster is a godsend. Do you want to release a production-level app or do you want to mess around? If it's the former, rest assured that almost every developer that has well-regarded apps in the Play Store uses libraries to make their lives easier. If it's the latter, feel free to mess around. But stay off my lawn!

The Nitty-Gritty

Time to get started!

First, go to https://developer.android.com/studio/index.html and download Android Studio. Android Studio is the official IDE for developing applications for Android and it does a lot of the heavy lifting for you.

Before you even write a single line of code, you should know that there are two files, called **AndroidManifest.xml** and **build.gradle** that you will be editing quite a lot but which contain no executable code for your application. Android Studio will set them up for you when you select "Create New Android Project" and follow the prompts, but we will be taking a look into them here. They will also be mentioned a lot in the rest of the book.

AndroidManifest.xml

The AndroidManifest.xml file contains **metadata** about your application. That's how almost every book and tutorial I've read and watched describe this (very important) file. What this *actually* means is that it does not contain any code but, instead, it contains things that are relevant to your application in various other ways like

- your app's unique package name
- your app's requested permissions
- whether your app needs access to specific hardware for it to run, eg the camera
- all Android components (remember those Activity, Service, Broadcast Receiver and Content Provider classes?) that are a part of your application. Broadcast receivers are an exception, since, depending on the circumstances, sometimes you won't declare them in the AndroidManifest
- more stuff

Usual Pitfalls, The Movie

If you ask Android Studio to create a new activity for you, it will also add an entry about that activity in your AndroidManifest.xml. If you don't ask Android Studio to create an activity for you, but instead create a class that extends Activity yourself, you will have to add an `<activity />` tag in the manifest! If you don't, and then try to launch that activity (which you'll learn how to do shortly), you app will crash.

This is NOT the actual pitfall, though. You will figure it out by googling in a minute (faster, if you check out the **stack trace**, which is essentially a log of sadness detailing how you fucked up).

The real trouble begins when you forget to add an entry for a service in `AndroidManifest.xml`. When you try to start that service, the application won't crash **but the service won't run** either, which is far worse.

At least by crashing it's letting you know that something is wrong. I once spent hours trying to figure out what was wrong, *even though I had known for quite some time that a service subclass has to be declared in the manifest.*

`build.gradle`

Android Studio uses the Gradle build system. Gradle automates the process of compiling your source code into an Android Package file (.apk), which is what you install on an actual device.

In the `build.gradle` files (every Android Studio project has two of them, a project-level build.gradle file, which you won't be editing a lot, and a module-level `build.gradle` file, which you will almost definitely be editing if you are doing any project that's beyond trivial) you can also manage your project's dependencies, ie. external libraries (like Retrofit and Picasso that I've already mentioned) that you want to use in your project.

Straight from the official documentation

> *Android Studio projects contain a top-level project*
> *Gradle build file that allows you to add the configuration*
> *options common to all application modules in the*
> *project. Each application module also has its own*
> *build.gradle file for build settings specific to that*
> *module.*

"What are these modules you speak of?", I hear you say.

Modules, dude. You may have one module for the phone app and another module for an Android Wear device. Common configuration options go in the top-level build.gradle file. If the phone module needs to include a particular library, the dependency to that library is only included in the phone module's build.gradle file. Simple, right?

For the time being, consider `build.gradle` a place where you'll declare the libraries you want to use in your project. Each library comes with instructions on how to accomplish exactly that.

XML

XML: Layouts, Resources and Assets

When you download and run Android Studio, you'll be given the option to create a new project, among other things. Select "Create New Project" (or whatever its counterpart is in your version of Android Studio) and follow the prompts.

Once you choose a project name and a company domain, Android Studio will generate a package name for you.

Click Next and you'll see a dialog that lets you select a minimum SDK level (the earliest version of Android your application will be able to run on). Select API 19 or 21 and check "Phone and Tablet" and, again, click "Next"

On the next screen, select "Empty Activity". Android Studio offers various templates for Activity styles but we want to start from scratch. After you've selected "Empty Activity", do what nobody expects you to do and click "Next" again.

The next and final screen lets you name your Activity and its associated layout file. Do not change anything. It'll suggest MainActivity as the name of the Activity and activity_main as the layout file. Click "Finish".

The `activity_main.xml` file

The activity_main.xml file is the layout file. This file contains, essentially, visual information, so there are two ways to see it: you can look at the source code or at a visual representation of it by clicking on "text" or "design" respectively at the bottom of the tab.
Maybe you'd like to play around with the visual editor for a bit. Drag and drop some widgets on the screen and resize them. Have some fun, I won't judge you.

Had your fun? Good. Now close it and forget that it ever existed.

Look, I'm not saying that it's crap. It has come a long way since the Eclipse/ADT days (you don't want to know). However, you will soon find out that working in XML is much easier and (more importantly) way more predictable. Working with nested layouts can be a huge pain.

So, XML on Android then. Let's start with a very important distinction.

Views and ViewGroups

From the Android Developer docs about the View class

*This class represents the basic building block for user interface components. **A View occupies a rectangular area on the screen** and is responsible for drawing and event handling. View is the base class for widgets, which are used to create interactive UI components (buttons, text fields, etc.). **The ViewGroup subclass is the base class for layouts, which are invisible containers that hold other Views** (or other ViewGroups) and define their layout properties.*

So, to repeat, just a little more plainly this time: a View takes up a rectangular area on the screen and is the basic building block for your user interface. **Views are also responsible for handling events, which I would super-bold, if super-bolding was a thing!**

A ViewGroup is used to group Views together. There are various subclasses of Views and ViewGroups with specific functionalities. In this section we'll go through the most important ones.

Views

Remember your Java tutorials? View is a direct descendant of Object. View *extends* Object. View has a ton of subclasses that provide specific functionality (interestingly, ViewGroup is one of them but we'll come back to that later). Here are the ones you'll be using all the time and, believe it or not, most user interfaces can be built by using these View subclasses in conjunction with some ViewGroups.

View

Your basic View. Personally, I use plain Views to create dividers in user interfaces or any other sort of horizontal or vertical line I need. You can, of course, extend View yourself to create your own custom Views but that's outside the scope of this book.

TextView

A TextView holds text — that much is obvious from the name. However, what is not obvious is that, since Views are responsible for handling events, a TextView can also be used as, for example, a Button. Android actually has a Button view for you to use but I never use it. Instead, I use a TextView with a background. Don't be confused into thinking that only Buttons can be tapped, as I did for a week after getting into Android development. You can tap any View, as long as you set a *click listener* on it (more on this soon).

ImageView

No prizes for guessing what an ImageView does at this point.

EditText

An EditText is simply an input field. Know those input fields that ask you to enter your email and password? Those are EditTexts.

A Note on creating user interfaces in Java

At this point, I should point out that it is possible to build your user interface using Java code instead of XML. Just because it's possible doesn't mean you should do it. You know what else is possible? Using your hands to walk. Licking your coffee from a tray like a freaking cat. Listening to "Stairway To Heaven" backwards.

In addition to being a huge pain in the ass, creating your UI in Java would also mean that there is no separation between the logic and the presentation of your application. Having your user interface in XML and the logic of your app in Java means that you can change the look of the app by editing the XML and the behaviour of your app by editing the Java code

Adding and customizing Views

Adding Views

You are ready to add a View to your layout! Good for you. The first thing you should have is a ViewGroup to add your view to. Since we haven't talked about ViewGroups yet, I'll just go ahead and pretend we already have one in our layout.

If you have ever worked with HTML on the web before, you'll be familiar with the concept of elements. In a webpage, that element could be a title, a paragraph, a header etc. On Android, something really similar happens. So, how is an element constructed?

An element is created by using a left-pointing angle bracket (<).

If we are adding a TextView, we'll do this

```
<TextView
```

Our job is not done yet!
When using XML, all elements must have a closing tag!
A closing tag includes the slash (/) character and a right-pointing angle bracket (>)

So, here is how a complete TextView element is declared, using an opening and closing tag

```
<TextView />
```

It is also legal for you to use the following syntax for declaring an element (and sometimes when using ViewGroups you will have no choice)

```
<TextView ></TextView>
```

Note that the closing tag is separate to the opening tag but you now have to type TextView twice, which sucks several kinds of balls.

Awesome! You have a complete TextView element declared in your XML. Now let's run this mother! Actually, let's not because it's going to crash. Why?

One thing you have to remember is that any view declared in XML on Android must have a width and height attribute declared! If you fail to add those two attributes, your app will crash.

Let's add those two attributes

```
<TextView
```

```
android:layout_width="match_parent"
android:layout_height="wrap_content"/>
```

To declare attributes in an XML element, you first use the
namespace prefix, in this case "android". In XML, a namespace
is a way to avoid element name conflicts. More on namespaces
(but not a whole lot more) and how to declare one in the
ViewGroup discussion.

After declaring the namespace ("android:"), you must then
specify the attribute you're interested in. In this case, it is the
width and the *height*. So how come you also have to add
"layout_" before specifying the width and the height?
android:width="something" makes much more sense, right?

Well, no. Using the **layout_** qualifier is a way for us to declare
**that the attribute we are specifying is meant for use by the
ViewGroup that contains the element and not the element itself.**

What?

Ok, let's make this clearer. Notice that when specifying the
width of the TextView in the example above, we used the value
"match_parent" instead of a numeric value (eg. 120 pixels)?

 "match_parent" is a special kind of value that means "make
the view as big in this dimension as the layout that contains it".

"`wrap_content`" is another special kind of value that means "make the view as big as it needs to be in order for its content to be able to fit in it".

A Note on Dimension Measurements in Android

*`android:layout_width` and `android:layout_height` and various other dimension- and position- related attributes can have their dimensions set in various units, like px (pixels), in (inches), mm (millimeters) but **you should always prefer the dp (density-independent pixels) unit**, unless you're specifying **text size**, in which case you should use **the sp (scaled pixels) unit**, for accessibility purposes.*

*Using density-independent pixels ensures that your application's elements will appear roughly equal-sized on screens with a wild variance in pixel density. **You don't want that 5mm line on your Nexus 4 be 1mm long on a Nexus 6P!** Using dp as a measurement unit will prevent this from happening.*

Here is what the official docs have to say about it, and for once they are not too cryptic

> *The density-independent pixel is equivalent to one physical pixel on a 160 dpi screen, which is the baseline density assumed by the system for a "medium" density screen. At*

runtime, the system transparently handles any scaling of the dp units, as necessary, based on the actual density of the screen in use. The conversion of dp units to screen pixels is simple: px = dp * (dpi / 160). For example, on a 240 dpi screen, 1 dp equals 1.5 physical pixels. You should always use dp units when defining your application's UI, to ensure proper display of your UI on screens with different densities.

So if your TextView is part of a ViewGroup, and that ViewGroup has a width of 120 pixels, that means that doing this

```
<TextView android:layout_width="match_parent"
     android:layout_height="wrap_content" />
```

will also make the TextView 120 pixels wide. This is why we say that the attribute is a hint for the ViewGroup that contains the element.

So, what is an example of an attribute that relates only to the element itself and not the containing layout? Great question.

Take a look at this

```
<TextView android:layout_width="match_parent"
    android:layout_height="wrap_content"
    android:textColor="#000000" />
```

See the **android:textColor** attribute? The color of the text does not concern the ViewGroup in the slightest (why would it?) so there is no layout_ qualifier added to it.

The android:textColor attribute is a nice segue into discussing the various way in which you can customize your views.

Customizing Views

Every type of view has several attributes that you can use in order to change something about that view's appearance (and positioning, but we will be discussing positioning in the ViewGroup section). I am now going to go through the attributes I use most often, since they are the ones you'll be most likely to use yourself too.

The one attribute you'll be using all the time

One attribute you'll be using constantly is the

android:id

attribute. The android:id attribute allows you to specify an id for your view so that you can refer to it later in other parts of your XML layout or in your Java code.
When you want to assign an id to a view, you go

```
android:id="@+id/id_name"
```

This will come in handy later. *Very* handy, in fact, so learn it by heart.

TextView

- *android:layout_width* & *android:layout_height*

Already discussed. Make sure to always use dp units when entering numeric values, unless you have a really good reason to not do so. So, for example, you'd use something like **android:layout_width="120dp"** and NOT **android:layout_width="120px"**

- *android:text="some text"*

I mean, come on, you know what this does! Just replace some text with your text. You can also refer to a string resource. More about resources later.

- *android:textColor="#FFFFFF"*

This attribute changes the contained text's color. You can provide the color by using hex notation (eg. #FFFFFF, which stands for white) or by referring to a color resource. Resources are something we will be discussing later in this book.

- *android:fontFamily*

This allows you to select from a (limited) number of font families. Depending on API level, valid values include "sans-serif", "sans-serif-condensed", "sans-serif-light", "sans-serif-thin" and "sans-serif-medium".

You can also combines these font families with the textStyle attribute to create various effects. So, coming up...

- *android:textStyle*

You can use the values "normal", "**bold**" and "*italic*" here (see what I did there?).

 Keep in mind that this works only with the included families mentioned above. If you use a custom typeface in your app (by eg. using the textView.setTypeface(typeface) method) on a TextView, asking the TextView in the XML to be in italic WILL NOT work. This makes sense, of course, because how would Android know where to find the font file for the italic version of the custom font you have used?

- *android:textSize*

This allows you to add a 'boink!' sound effect when your TextView is clicked.
NOT REALLY! But you should have seen your face! Naturally, this lets you specify the size of your text. Always prefer to set your text size using **sp** units (scaled pixel), since this will allow

your text to scale according to what the user has chosen in the accessibility settings.

So, do this: **android:textSize="14sp"**.

NOT this: **android:textSize="14dp"**

ImageView

The most important ImageView-specific attribute (especially if you're displaying bitmaps) is, in my opinion

- *android:scaleType="centerCrop"*

Valid values for the *scaleType* attribute are

fitXY: Use if you want your app to look like **ass**. And I don't even mean the good kind of ass but more like the hairy, disgusting type of ass. What **fitXY** does is stretch the image to fit exactly in the dimensions of the ImageView.

Imagine the you have a landscape photo but your ImageView is taller than it is wide. The photo will be shown in its entirety but it will be horribly squashed, so that the entire thing fits into a portrait-orientation (essentially) ImageView. Were you a fan of Geocities-made websites in the 90s? Then you'll love this scale type. Don't know what I'm talking about? Consider yourself lucky.

I have already petitioned to change the name of this type to "horror" but

```
android:scaleType="horror"
```

probably doesn't look too appealing. It's more descriptive, though.

I don't know if there are any actual reasons for someone to use this but if there are, I haven't found them yet.

Enough `fitXY` hate. Let's move on.

center: This attribute will perform no scaling but will center the image in the ImageView. This is pretty cool when you don't care which part of the image will be shown to a user or simply want to give the user a general idea about the image but displaying it fully is not necessary. For example, if the ImageView is used as a thumbnail that doesn't need to contain the entire image, you could use this scale type. No scaling also means that there will be no distortion of the image.

Be warned that no scaling also means that if the image is smaller in dimensions than its ImageView container (eg. the image is 30px*30px and the container is 50px*50px), the image will not fill the container. If it is bigger, the container will be filled.

`centerInside:` This attribute will scale the image to fit inside the ImageView, while keeping the aspect ratio of the image. The difference with the `center` attribute only becomes obvious when the image is larger than its ImageView container: using `centerInside`, the image will be resized so that the entirety of it fits inside the container. In the case of plain `center,` you will see part of the image displayed (its center portion) but the rest of the image will be clipped because it will be outside the bounds of the ImageView.

`centerCrop:` Oh my, another **centerSomething** attribute. This is actually my favorite scale type (that's a sentence I never thought I'd say) for design-related tasks: if I don't care about showing the entirety of the image but only want to use an image to *make something look pretty*, this will do the job perfectly. centerCrop will scale the image so that both axes are equal or bigger than that the axes of the container and then center the scaled image.

`fitCenter:` What, more center stuff? You bet. `fitCenter` scales the image so that it fits inside the container, with one of its axes exactly matching the containing ImageView. Then it centers the image in the ImageView.

fitStart: `fitStart` will scale the image in the exact same way as `fitCenter` (ie. make it fit inside the container with one of its axes matching the size of the container exactly) but then instead of centering it inside the ImageView container, it will place it on the top left of the ImageView.

fitEnd: `fitEnd` will scale the image in the exact same way that it would using `fitCenter` or `fitStart`, but after scaling the image it will place it in the bottom right of the container.

matrix: while this sounds all kinds of exciting, your image will not be dodging bullets in slow motion, Neo. **matrix** allows you use a Matrix class to manipulate the image, to eg. scale or rotate it before it is displayed on the ImageView. You can provide the Matrix object by calling **.setImageMatrix()** on the ImageView object in code. I would suggest that you forget about it for the time being.

Oh, dang! These are a lot of scale types!

Yes, they are. The best way to see how they work is to just use them for yourself and see the results.

However, I have to reiterate that, for most tasks, **centerCrop** *is still my favorite. As long as you make sure that your images are of high enough resolution, your ImageView will always appear filled, with no nasty gaps between the ImageView and the rest of your content.*

- `android:src="@drawable/source_file"`

It goes without saying that, when you want to load an image in an ImageView, you have to specify a source file for that image. This is what `android:src` achieves.

The source file of the image should be in your **res/drawable** or **res/drawable**-withqualifiers folder (I'll come back to the qualifiers things later in the Resources section). After specifying the `@drawable` part, you enter a slash character and then the name of the image file *without an extension*. And there you go: the image is in your ImageView. Good job, even if a monkey could do it.

What happens if you don't specify the `android:src` attribute? Nothing, but there will be no image in your ImageView, it'll just be empty space. Will you even need to do this?

Maybe. Sometimes, you don't want to show anything until an image is, say, downloaded from the web (and even in that case, I'd still use an image as a placeholder). So you don't define the source file and you load an image when it's downloaded *programmatically (*which means that you do it later in code*).*

EditText

In addition to everything you can use on a TextView, EditText provides you with the following important attributes

- *android:hint="your hint here"*

Let's say that you want a user to enter their name in your EditText. How do they know that it is their name that they have to enter? You can use a label, I guess — if you want other designers to say "2001 called. It wants its design pattern back". Those bastards.

By passing a string into `android:hint`, the EditText will display it to inform the user about the sort of information you want them to enter in that specific field. As soon as the user taps the EditText, "poof!" goes the hint! The EditText is cleared and the user can enter the required information.

- *android:inputType="type"*

This attribute will let you select the sort of keyboard that appears when the user taps the EditText or even modify the text entered into the EditText. There are a lot of parameters that can be passed as an inputType but one of the most important is

android:inputType="textPassword"

which will mask the characters the user enters as a password (it will show dots instead of the actual characters).

Another interesting one is

android:inputType="number"

which will force the numeric-only keyboard to pop up. Users won't be even able to enter text into this field, which is neat and also saves you the trouble of validating the input.

You can find an exhaustive list of inputType attributes at https://developer.android.com/reference/android/widget/TextView.html#attr_android:inputType

Common View attributes

In addition to specialized attributes for each View subclass, there are shared attributes that are inherited from the base View class that can be used on every View type. These are the attributes I most commonly use

- *android:background*

This attribute lets you change the background color of the view or even use an image as the background. You can even create a tiled background, by repeating the same image ("tile"). The latter case requires you to create a `<bitmap />` drawable XML file and it's not something you'll be doing often (I've never done it in a production app) so disregard it for now.

Setting the background color is really easy. Just do this

```
android:background="#FFCCAA"
```

The color can be specified as a resource (more on resources later) or in a hexadecimal format, as done above.

If you want to set a picture as a background, do this

```
android:background="@drawable/image_fil
e_name"
```

You will notice that the image file to be used as a background is specified by using the prefix **@drawable**, followed by a slash and the name of the image file. You are still fresh, young padawan, but this is an example of using a resource. Any attribute specified by having a @ character preceding it means that you are referring to a resource, which is essentially a piece of content saved in the **res/** directory of your project.
@drawable will refer to an image file in one of (possibly) many **res/drawable/** folders in your project.
Again, we'll go into more detail on this in the resources section.

For now, two things:

1. The image file can be in .png, .jpg. .bmp, .gif or (in some API levels) .webp format

2. Be careful when using an image as a background for a view **directly**. Since you cannot use the scaleType attribute in this case (if your view is not an ImageView), the image will automatically scale so that the entire

image fits the view size (similar to `fitXY` we discussed above) and it will be distorted, making it look megacrappy. No, **ultra**crappy.

Because of the second point, I never use the `android:background` attribute to set a picture as a background for a view. Instead, I place an ImageView behind the view that should have the background, make the ImageView exactly the same size as the view and then load the picture in the ImageView by using its `android:src` attribute and a scale type of `android:scaleType="centerCrop"`.

- *android:padding*

Padding is essentially empty space *within* the border of the view itself. That is, surrounding the content of the view but not *around* the view.

Here's a (slightly macabre) example that'll help you remember the concept, with the added bonus of maybe haunting your nightmares forever: you are a person. You have a skeleton. Let's say that the skeleton is the view content. Your flesh around the skeleton is the padding (stay with me here) but you are still a single person. A unit. That's the relationship a view has with its padding.

Now, if another person comes along and (hopefully) keeps some distance from you, the distance between you is the margin (more on margins in a bit). Two different people separated by that distance. *Margin.*

Keep in mind that there are padding, paddingTop, paddingRight, paddingLeft and paddingBottom attributes that you can set separately if you want your padding to be uneven on different sides of the view. However, also note that if you do this

```
android:padding="8dp"
```

and then do this in the same view

```
android:paddingTop="16dp"
```

the second attribute (paddingTop) will NOT override the first one. Padding will stay at 8dp around the view. The way to actually give a padding of 16dp at the top and 8dp everywhere else is to, unfortunately, do this

```
android:paddingLeft="8dp"
android:paddingRight="8dp"
android:paddingBottom="8dp"
```

```
android:paddingTop="16dp"
```

The order doesn't matter but still, remember: **setting *android:padding* to a value and then setting a specific padding attribute to another value will not override the *android:padding* value**, no matter the order they are declared.

- *android:layout_margin*

The margin is the space between views that is not included in the views themselves. Let me explain the difference between margin and padding with an example: so, you have a skeleton. Joking. I already explained the difference above.

Interesting facts: notice that the margin attribute is preceded by the *layout_* modifier after the *android:* namespace declaration. Remember what is signified by this? A margin setting is meant for the container layout, not for the view itself.

Think about it: space that is included in the view itself should be of interest only to the view. And that's how it is — **android:padding**

However, the space between views is (as it should be) a direction for the container layout, since the space is not included in the views themselves.
Hence — **android:*layout_margin***

Similarly to padding, margin attributes come in more specific versions

```
android:layout_marginBottom
android:layout_marginTop
android:layout_marginLeft
android:layout_marginRight
```

Also similarly to padding, if you do this

```
android:layout_margin="8dp"
```

and then do this

```
android:layout_marginTop="16dp"
```

the more specific attribute (`marginTop`) **will not override** the more general attribute, no matter the ordering of the declarations (ie. whether `layout_marginTop` is declared first or after `layout_margin`). To specify different margins for different sides of the view, you'll have to forego using the general attribute and stick to using the specific ones.

Which is a huge `layout_pain` in the `layout_ass`. I agree.

- *android:elevation*

This is an awesome attribute that was added in API 21 (Lollipop). Elevation makes your views appear raised by casting a shadow behind them. This can make your layouts appear more natural and I'm definitely an advocate of using it.

Elevation is best defined in (again) density-independent pixels (dp). The highest the number, the more diffused the shadow to give the appearance of the view being higher.

What most guides will not tell you (but this one will, good choice!) is that, **if you haven't set a background to your view, you won't get any visible elevation.** Which makes sense, I guess, in a physics-respecting way (a transparent element should cast no shadow) but it's still maddening until you discover it.

So doing this

```
<TextView
    android:layout_width="64dp"
    android:layout_height="64dp"
    android:text="hello, you"
```

```
                 android:elevation="8dp" />
```

will not add a shadow to your view.

Doing **this** will

```
          <TextView
              android:layout_width="64dp"
              android:layout_height="64dp"
              android:text="hello, you"
              android:elevation="8dp"
              android:background="#eeeeee" />
```

The background is no longer transparent. It has a color (#eeeeee), so it will cast a shadow. Your view will now have a shadow to indicate that it is raised. Good job, me!

ViewGroups

At last, we get to the missing piece of creating your very own layouts!

ViewGroups are, as I have already mentioned, containers that can contain views. Maybe you're thinking "why would I need different kinds of container? Shouldn't one type of container suffice?".

Well, no. Different types of containers have different attributes available to them that work better for certain kinds of situations. I will mention the ones I use most often because, while there are others, these will enable you to create almost everything you'd ever want to use.

Let's start with...

LinearLayout

As its name implies, a LinearLayout places the views it contains in a linear arrangement. That is, one after another. That's why one of its most important attributes is

- *android:orientation*

which can either be **vertical** or **horizontal**.

Let's see an example

```
<LinearLayout
    android:layout_width="match_parent"
    android:layout_height="match_parent"
    android:orientation="horizontal">

</LinearLayout>
```

Here, we have a LinearLayout that is as big as its parent in width and height (which also means that, if this layout is the *root* layout, it will take up the entirety of the screen) and that will place its views horizontally.

Notice that I have split the LinearLayout declaration into an **opening tag** that doesn't immediately close (<LinearLayout >) but that is closed later (</LinearLayout>). **The layout's attributes are defined in the opening tag section. The views that we want to add to the layout are placed between the opening tag and the closing tag.**

If you do this (don't do this)

```
<LinearLayout

    android:layout_width="match_parent"
    android:layout_height="match_parent"
    android:orientation="horizontal" />
```

it will not be invalid but will have nowhere to place your views. What a dumbass. This used to be me. Shudder.

Ok, let's place a couple of views in the layout

```xml
<LinearLayout

    android:layout_width="match_parent"
    android:layout_height="match_parent"
    android:orientation="horizontal">
    <TextView
        android:layout_width="100dp"
        android:layout_height="wrap_content"
        android:text="hi, I'm the best textview!"
      />
      <TextView
        android:layout_width="100dp"
        android:layout_height="wrap_content"
        android:text="lol, not even close" />
</LinearLayout>
```

Pop quiz time! How do you think these two views will appear on the screen?

1. They will appear next to each other
2. The first TextView will be on top and the second TextView will appear below it
3. Shit, I don't know, son. Who do you think I am, Erwin Einstein?

Obviously, they will appear next to each other! That's what horizontal means, right? If you specify a vertical orientation, they will appear in a column, with the first TextView on top of the second one. The order matters. If you add a third TextView (or any other view), it will appear below the second one. Easy, right?

But what happens if you don't specify the layout's orientation? **The views will be arranged in the default orientation, which is horizontal.**

Another thing to keep in mind: a LinearLayout will create a single row (in horizontal orientation) or column (in vertical orientation) of views. Don't be confused if you have two views in a horizontal LinearLayout and one of them is invisible: chances are that the second one is off-screen, on the right of the first one. If, for example, the first view has *android:layout_width* set to **match_parent,** it will take the entirety of the screen's width and any other views in that layout will be outside the bounds of the screen, hence invisible.

- *android:weightSum*

Ooh, I love this one and it's corresponding childrens' attribute *android:layout_weight.*

It's also really easy to understand. Let's say that you have a horizontal LinearLayout and you want to add three children. You want these children to be equal in width.

Let's go with three ImageViews in a horizontal linear layout (continues on next page)

```
<LinearLayout
    android:layout_height="wrap_content"
    android:layout_width="match_parent"
    android:weightSum="3"
    android:orientation="horizontal">

        <ImageView
                android:layout_width="0dp"
                android:layout_weight="1"

        android:layout_height="96dp"

        android:scaleType="centerCrop"

        android:src="@drawable/image1"/>
        <ImageView
                android:layout_width="0dp"
                android:layout_weight="1"

        android:layout_height="96dp"

        android:scaleType="centerCrop"

        android:src="@drawable/image2"/>
        <ImageView
```

```
            android:layout_width="0dp"
            android:layout_weight="1"

        android:layout_height="96dp"

        android:scaleType="centerCrop"

        android:src="@drawable/image3" />

    </LinearLayout>
```

Yikes! *android:layout_width="0dp"*? Seriously?

Yep. This is very important to understand.

When you do the *weightSum* and *layout_weight* thingy, you are letting the framework take care of the dimension you're interested in for you. Your instructions tell the layout "split the width of the layout in three (since the orientation is horizontal the weight attributes are going to affect the horizontal dimension) and place three equally-sized (width-wise) ImageViews in it".

So you specifying a width doesn't make any sense. Problem is, if you don't specify a width (remember, it's mandatory for any view), Android's gonna slap you IN DA FACE and your app is going to crash. So you specify the width as "0" and Android figures out the width for you! Clear? Good.

Now, if the orientation was vertical, you'd let the layout take care of the vertical dimension (ie. the height) for you. So in that case, you'd specify the width normally and then you'd set the `android:layout_height` attribute to 0dp.

Another interesting fact is that you can omit setting a *weightSum* attribute on the layout. *The layout_weight attribute is relative:* in the above example, you could have set `android:layout_weight="3"` on all three ImageViews and the layout's width would still be split evenly. Or "4". Or "5". As long as you used the same number, the width would again be split evenly.

If, however, you set `android:layout_weight` equal to **1** on the first ImageView, then **2** on the second ImageView and then **4** in the third ImageView, the first ImageView would take 1/7th of the layout's width, the second ImageView would take 2/7ths of the layout's width and the third ImageView would take 4/7th of the layout's width.

I always try to use a *weightSum* attribute in the parent layout, though, just to keep things readable.

RelativeLayout

RelativeLayout is *awesome*. Seriously, I'm in love with it. It's a super-flexible layout that allows your UI to be more responsive to different screen sizes, among other things.

Here is a very clear (for a change) explanation from the Android developer docs

> *A Layout where the positions of the children can be described in relation to each other or to the parent*

If this still sounds a bit cryptic to you, don't worry: everything will be cleared up soon.

In a RelativeLayout, if you want a TextView to be at the top and on the right side of the layout, you simply tell it to go there. If you another view to be to the left of that TextView, you again tell it to go there. The way you give these instructions to the views is (of course) by using XML attributes. Let's see how it works.

- *android:layout_alignParentTop = "true" / "false"*

This tells a view to go to the top of the parent layout (if set to true, obviously). No prizes for guessing what

- `android:layout_alignParentBottom`
- `android:layout_alignParentLeft`

&

- `android:layout_alignParentRight`

do.

- `android:layout_centerHorizontal="true" /` `"false"`

This centers the view horizontally into the parent layout. Its twin

- `android:layout_centerVertical ="true" /` `"false"`

centers the view vertically into the parent layout.

It goes without saying that setting both of those to "true" will place the view smack bang in the middle (center) of the layout. But wait! There's a shortcut! If you want to center a view in the layout, in both the vertical and the horizontal dimension, you can simply go

- `android:layout_centerInParent="true"`

and you're done. Enjoy these small luxuries, because the Android SDK won't afford them to you very often. Bad SDK!

- *android:layout_above*

So you want your view to be positioned above another view? [telemarketer voice] *With this simple attribute, you can move your view on top of any other view!* [/telemarketer voice]

Remember the huge, full-page line, asking you to learn by heart how to set a view's id in XML? Let's recap. When you create a view, you can give it an id by doing the following

```
<View
    android:layout_height="wrap_content"
    android:layout_width="wrap_content"
    android:id="@+id/my_view" />
```

See the bolded part? That's the line where the view's id is set. In this case, it's "my_view".

The reason you're giving your views an id (even though you're not required to do so and the app will compile normally with no errors if you don't give your view an id) is *so you can refer to that view later in your XML document or Java code.*

We have reached the part where you want to refer to this view. Why? You want to say that another view should be placed above it! So, what you do is this

```
<View
    android:layout_height="wrap_content"
    android:layout_width="wrap_content"
    android:id="@+id/my_view" />

<View
    android:layout_height="wrap_content"
    android:layout_width="wrap_content"
    android:id="@+id/my_other_view"
    android:layout_above="@id/my_view" />
```

This will place "my_other_view" above "my_view" in a RelativeLayout.

Three things to notice:

1. When you refer to another view, you don't use the "+" sign. When giving a view an id, you go `android:id="@+id/view_id"`. When referring to another view, you omit the "+" sign, so you do this: `android:layout_above="@id/view_id"`. Remember that the "+" sign is used when assigning an id to a view

(it makes sense: since you're creating a new id, you're adding it).

2. **This will only place "my_other_view" above "my_view" if the parent layout is a RelativeLayout**. Obviously, if you're using another type of layout, your app will not compile, since other layouts do not allow the `android:layout_above` attribute to be used in their children. Good parenting or a reason for child views to rebel when they reach puberty? Your opinion matters.

3. If you want a view to be place above another view, you have to be careful with the ordering. Let's make this more general, in fact: if you want to refer to another view, make sure that the view you're referring to precedes the view in which you're referring to that view. To make it more clear, **if you want to refer to view1 in view2 for any reason, view1 has to be declared before view2 in the layout.** The following example will crash and burn

```
<RelativeLayout
    android:layout_width="match_parent"
    android:layout_height="match_parent">
```

```
<View
    android:layout_width="wrap_content"
    android:layout_height="wrap_content"
    android:id="@+id/view1"
    android:layout_above="@id/view2" />

<View
    android:layout_width="wrap_content"
    android:layout_height="wrap_content"
    android:id="@+id/view2"/>
</RelativeLayout>
```

Why? You are trying (well, I am) to refer to view2 in view1, **when view2 hasn't been declared yet in the layout**. It is declared after view1.

One last thing: placing a view above another view does not mean that it will be placed above it horizontally too. For example, if a view is centered horizontally by using the android:layout_centerHorizontal="true" attribute and then declared that another view should be placed above it, the second view will be placed above it but it will not be centered horizontally.

If you want the second view to be above the first view and centered horizontally, you have to explicitly declare it in the second view too. Otherwise, the second view will be placed above the first view, but on the top left of the screen.

- *android:layout_below*

Just like `android:layout_above`, but this one places the view below the one it is referring to. Usage is exactly the same.

- *android:layout_toLeftOf*

Want to guess what this does? You must have gotten the hang of it so far! That's right — provide it with a view id and watch your view be placed to the left of the referred view. Simply put

```
<RelativeLayout … >

    <View
        android:id="@+id/view1"
        android:layout_width="wrap_content"
        android:layout_height="wrap_content" />

    <View
        android:id="@+id/view2"
        android:layout_width="wrap_content"
        android:layout_height="wrap_content"
        android:layout_toLeftOf="@id/view1" />
```

```
</RelativeLayout>
```

This will place **view2** to the left of **view1. Again, don't be confused when view2 is placed to the left of view1 but (potentially) on a different vertical position. This code ONLY guarantees that view2 will be placed on the left of view1.**

For example, if view1 also contained the attribute

```
android:layout_centerVertical="true"
```

view2 would be placed on it's left but it wouldn't be centered vertically too. view2 would be placed on view1's left but on the top (start) of the layout, since by default, all views are placed on the top left of a Relative Layout.

When we specify a horizontal position, like android:layout_toLeftOf does, we override the default horizontal position but we do not override the default vertical position!

If we wanted view2 to be placed on view1's left AND on the same vertical position, we'd also have to specify

```
android:layout_centerVertical="tru
e"
```

in view2 too.

- *android:layout_toRightOf*

Exactly like android:layout_toLeftOf. But on the right.

- *android:layout_alignBaseline*

This is also pretty simple: provide a view id to this attribute so that your view's baseline aligns to the baseline of the referred view.

FrameLayout

From the Android developer docs

> *FrameLayout is designed to block out an area on the screen to display a single item.*

As you can see, the Android developer docs suggest that it should generally hold only one child view because it's difficult to organize multiple child views in a responsive manner (ie. in devices with different screen sizes, the child views may end up overlapping each other).

I sometimes use a FrameLayout to stack views on top of each other. For example, if I want to have a photo as a background, another semi-transparent layer on top of it and then text on top of both of them, I would use a FrameLayout, even if a RelativeLayout would also do the job. Keep in mind that a RelativeLayout is a heavier, more computationally expensive layout than a FrameLayout.

A point I should have made earlier is that views placed on a layout in Android follow z-ordering. Because z-order probably sounds like a cult to you (The Order of the Z!), it simply describes the way views are placed back to front on a screen.

Views declared earlier in an XML layout (closer to the top of the document) are placed "deeper" (essentially underneath) than views declared later (closer to the bottom of the document).

That means that if I, for example, place two identically sized views in the center of a layout in this way

```
<RelativeLayout … >
    <TextView
        android:id="@+id/view_one"
        android:text="hey there!"
        android:layout_width="200dp"
        android:layout_height="64dp"
        android:layout_centerInParent="true" />

    <TextView
        android:id="@+id/view_two"
        android:text="hey tharr!"
        android:layout_width="200dp"
        android:layout_height="64dp"
        android:layout_centerInParent="true" />
</RelativeLayout>
```

only the pirate-inspired version, view_two, ("hey tharr!") will be visible, since it is declared later in the layout, hence it will be placed on top of view_one. Since they are the same size, view_two will be completely blocking view_one.

There is an exception to this rule: if you use the *android:elevation* attribute to give view_one a higher elevation than view_two, view_one will block view_two instead, since it will be placed "higher" relative to view_two.

ScrollView

A ScrollView is a layout container that allows vertical scrolling, in case the contained view or layout contains more content than the screen can display.

The only ScrollView-specific layout attribute is

- *android:fillViewport*

which forces the ScrollView to stretch its contents to fill the viewport.

Set this value to "true" if you value your sanity. "false" is what Abdul Alhazred used right before he went mad and wrote the Necronomicon. You have been warned.

A very important thing to remember is that a ScrollView should only have one direct child.

This does not mean that you can only place one layout or view in a ScrollView. Just that the ScrollView itself can only have one child. For example, here

```
<ScrollView
    android:layout_width="match_parent"
    android:layout_height="match_parent" >
    <RelativeLayout … >
    </RelativeLayout>
</ScrollView>
```

the ScrollView only has one direct child (the RelativeLayout) but go ahead and **nest** all the layouts you want inside the RelativeLayout!

Hey, wait a moment! Did I even explain what *nesting* is?

A Note on Nesting

Nesting refers to the act of placing layouts inside other layouts. For example, if you place a LinearLayout inside a RelativeLayout, the LinearLayout is nested inside the RelativeLayout. You can go further and nest another RelativeLayout (or any layout, really) inside the

LinearLayout for complex view hierarchies. Just be warned that deep levels of nesting can cause performance problems.

One last thing: the root layout (the one in which all other layouts or views are contained) in an Android XML layout file must contain a namespace declaration. Here is a root RelativeLayout and the namespace declaration in bold

```
<RelativeLayout

xmlns:android="http://schemas.android.com/ap
k/res/android"
    android:layout_width="match_parent"
    android:layout_height="match_parent" >

</RelativeLayout>
```

Also, the start of an XML file should contain an XML declaration. Putting it all together, this is how an XML document with a root RelativeLayout should look like (the XML declaration is bolded)

```
<?xml version="1.0" encoding="utf-8"?>
<RelativeLayout

xmlns:android="http://schemas.android.com/ap
k/res/android"
    android:layout_width="match_parent"
    android:layout_height="match_parent" >

</RelativeLayout>
```

AdapterViews

I'll try to be as clear as I can, because I was a bit confused with what an AdapterView is at first. The concept is really clear, once you've had an example described to you.

Let's say that you have an ArrayList (a class that's part of the Java Collection framework) of persons (or, if you want to be all Java about it, ArrayList<Person>). Each person has some properties you can set, like their name, age and address.

Now, you want to take this collection of persons and present it to a user as a list they can read. **An AdapterView is a view that is able to display this list of persons.**

How does an AdapterView display this list of persons? It does not happen directly. Before the list of persons can be fed into an AdapterView to be displayed, it has to go through something called an **Adapter**, which will format the objects appropriately for visual representation.

These are the steps

1. You have your list of objects that you want to display to a user
2. You feed this list of objects to an adapter

3. You set the adapter on the AdapterView

This is some simplified code about how you would do this

```
ArrayList<Person> persons = new
ArrayList<Person>();

Person person1 = new Person("Jake", 23,
"21 Elm Street");

Person person2 = new Person("Tim", 45,
"19 Arlington Street");

persons.add(person1);
persons.add(person2);

// ok, we have our collection of two
persons
// now let's create an adapter object
by feeding the persons
// arraylist into the adapter

PersonAdapter adapter = new
PersonAdapter(persons);
```

```
// now let's set the adapter on the
adapterview

adapterView.setAdapter(adapter);

// now let's have some tequila, baby!
```

You're probably thinking "what's a PersonAdapter and how do I create one?" which is not within the scope of this book. The Android SDK has a pretty simple ArrayAdapter that you can use for simple situations, like displaying text.

Let's see how you can use it

```
ArrayList<String> names = new
ArrayList<String>();

// … and add some names to it

names.add("Jack");
names.add("Jill");
names.add("Tom");
names.add("Jerry");

// let's create the adapter
```

```
ArrayAdapter<String> adapter = new
ArrayAdapter<String>(context,
android.R.layout.simple_list_item_1, names);


listView.setAdapter(adapter);
```

This code will display the names in a list. *listView* in this example is an instance of a **ListView** (you will find out how to create this instance soon). A ListView presents data in a vertically scrolling list.

Another kind of AdapterView is a **GridView**, which is an AdapterView that presents data in a grid.

More AdapterViews? Sure! A **Spinner** is an AdapterView that presents data in a drop-down list when tapped.

The ArrayAdapter class has a variety of constructors (remember those?) and in the example above we're using the simplest one. It takes three arguments

1. **context**: this is the current Context. What is the Context? Here is the best explanation I could find, courtesy of <u>some awesome person on StackOverflow</u>

As the name suggests, it's the context of current state of the application/object. It lets newly-created objects understand what has been going on.

"Context is there to provide orientation for newly-created objects and describes the environment they find themselves in" is actually the way I would put it.

Activity and Service (two out of the four Android app components) are Context subclasses and they inherit a bunch of methods from it. You'll hear more about Context in the rest of this book.

2. **`android.R.layout.simple_list_item_1`**: ok, I'll come back to this after bullet point 3, because this is super-important!

3. **names**: the collection of names that will appear in the AdapterView.

Ok, back to bullet point 2: this long-ass argument is actually an int (an argument of type integer). It looks very confusing to a newcomer to Android but it is simpler than it appears.

Let's break it down:

- **android.R**: this part of the argument refers to a framework resource. Surely this must clear things up for.

LOL! Of course it doesn't. A framework resource is a resource that comes as part of the OS. Something built-in to Android. But *what* is a resource? Great question. In the next chapter, you'll learn a lot about resources in Android but for now, let's just say that a resource is some piece of data that your app can access and use, often (but not always) defined in XML.

- **layout** : this specifies that the framework resource you're accessing is a layout resource. Again, read on to learn more about resources.

- **simple_list_item_1**: this specifies the exact layout you want to access. Want to see its source code? Here it is:

```
<TextView
xmlns:android="http://schemas.android.com/apk/res/
android"
    android:id="@android:id/text1"
    style="?android:attr/listItemFirstLineStyle"
    android:paddingTop="2dp"
    android:paddingBottom="3dp"
```

```
android:layout_width="match_parent"
android:layout_height="wrap_content" />
```

Remind you of anything? Other than the "style" attribute, it should look really familiar to you: it is just a TextView.

This TextView will display the text for each row in the ListView. One instance per list item. In the example above, "Jack" gets his own row and his own instance of a TextView. "Jill" also gets her own row and in turn her own instance of this TextView. And so on, until all names have been displayed as entries in the ListView.

In the next chapter we'll discuss one of the most important and powerful parts of Android development, Resources. Are you tired? Well, let me renew your interest by saying that **A Fledgling Android Developer Reads The Resources Chapter. You Won't Believe What Happens Next**.

Resources and R.java

What are Resources? Resources are essentially all the non-code (non-code includes your XML layouts, drawables etc) parts of your application.

XML layouts? Resources!
.png, .jpeg, .gif image files? Resources!
.wav, .mp3 sound files? Resources!
.mp4 videos? Resources!

Resources are put in a folder of your app's structure called **res/**, in various subfolders, depending on their format and intended purpose. The most often used subfolders in the /res folder are

`res/layout/`

this is where you (unsurprisingly) put your XML layout files. You can also have res/layout-withQualifier/ folders, like **res/layout-land/**, where you place your layouts that are meant to be displayed in landscape orientation and **res/layout-port/**, that are meant to be displayed when the user is drinking port wine. *Just kidding* — when the device is in portrait orientation.

`res/drawable/`

This is where you place your various image / drawable files. In Android, in addition to the usual bitmap image file formats, you can also define visual resources, such as ovals, rectangles, lines and rings, in XML. These also go in your res/drawable/ folder.

An Android app usually has various res/**drawable-qualifier** folders that contain assets for different screen densities. Qualifiers are a huge part of the Resources system, that allow you to control which resources will be used in specific devices or device configurations (for example, you can use an XML layout for when the device is in portrait and a completely different one for when the device is in landscape orientation).

Here are some examples of *drawable-qualifier*

`drawable/hdpi:` place files for devices with hdpi screen densities

`drawable/xxhdpi:` place files for devices with extra-extra-high density displays

Creating assets for screens of various densities can be a chore, so if your designer has not exported them for you (or if, more likely, you're also the designer), tools like Roman Nurik's Android Asset Studio at https://romannurik.github.io/AndroidAssetStudio/ can generate them for you.

Keep in mind that you can place all your drawables without any qualifier in the res/drawable (or any drawable-withQualifier folder) and Android will scale them up or down for you as required.
Be warned though that this brings with it a performance penalty (since scaling will have to be performed by the system) and that low-res images scaled up for high-density screens will look blurred and all sorts of crappy.

Personally, if I'm creating an MVP (minimum viable product) app I'll take all sorts of shortcuts, like using only high-resolution image files and let the framework handle the scaling down for me.

But I'll never use low-res image files and let the system scale them up for me because that's just nasty, man.

/res/raw

In this folder, you place various file types that your app can use, like .mp3 sounds files and .mp4 videos. Placing a file in the /res/raw folder will generate a *resource id* (an integer that's a unique identifier for this file) for it.

Pretty soon you'll learn what a resource id is and what you can use it for.

`/assets/`

This folder is *not* a resources folder. I'm just including it here since it contains files that are non-code assets of your application.

The `assets/` folder is not a subfolder of the `/res/` folder. It is included in your project in the same level as the `/res/` folder. Android Studio will generate an `/assets/` folder for you if you ask it nicely.

Files placed in the `assets/` folder will not have resource IDs generated for them and the way you access these files from code is different to how you'd access resources files.

I usually use the `assets/` folder for font files that I then access from my code.

`res/values/`

In the res/values/ folder, you place various values like strings, dimensions, colors etc. What are these values? Well, strings are just what you guessed: text meant to be used by your app.

Wait a minute, I hear you say. *Why not just put these strings straight into my code? Why do I have to define them in a res/values/ directory?*

Good question. Placing the text straight into your code prevents you from easily changing the text content in the future. Image that you have a string saying "Are you sure you want to proceed?" that's meant to be used in three different places in your application. Changing the string to "Are you certain that you want to proceed" would require you to change the text in three different places, if this text was hard-coded in your code. Not so with a string resource: just change it in one place and all of the text will be taken care of.

Same story with the dimensions resource: a dimensions resource will let you define a dimension in any unit you want (but as always, dp is always preferred) and re-use it all around your code. To be perfectly frank, I rarely use dimension resources (shame on me!), I just hardcode those values into my XML layouts.

I do use color resources constantly, though: when you decide what colors you want to use in your app, I strongly suggest that you create color resources that you can refer to. This will keep you using a defined color palette and be more consistent in your color choices.

Creating value resources is really simple. In your `/res/values/` folder, create an XML file that will contain your string resources. You could call this file `res/values/englishmuffin.xml` for all Android cares, but by convention the file is called **`strings.xml`**.

In `strings.xml`, open a resources tag and place the string resource inside, like this

```
<resources>
    <string name="app_name">Super
Awesome App!</string>
</resources>
```

This will create a resource id for the "Super Awesome App!" string, called **`R.string.app_name`**

Stick around for a little longer to see how you can access this string from your code or XML layouts.

Creating other sorts of resources is really similar: in a `<resources> </resources>` tag, for dimension resources do this

```
<resources>
    <dimen
name="cancel_button_padding">3dp</dimen
>
</resources>
```

This will create a resource id for this dimension of 3dp, called
R.dimen.cancel_button_padding

Finally, for a color resource do this

```
<resources>
    <color name="gray">#424242</color>
</resources>
```

This will create a color resource with a resource id of
R.color.gray

As with the `strings.xml` example, the convention is putting
dimension resources in a `/res/values/dimens.xml` file and
the color resources in a `res/values/colors.xml` file.

However, as was the case with string resources, you can call
these files anything you want. Just *don't*. Be helpful to the poor
developer that may be maintaining your code down the road.
When he or she comes looking, they'll be expecting you to
follow convention.

I will not cover any more resource types in this book, since these should be more than enough to get you started. What is important is for you to know that, like other resource types, **res/values/** folders support **qualifiers**. In fact, the accepted way of localizing your app in Android (show English text to devices that have their language set to English and German text that have their language set to German) is, again, using qualifiers!

In the example above, you'd do this by using two folders in **res/**. One would be called **res/values-en/** and would contain a strings.xml file with English text and the other would be called **res/values-de/** and would contain a `strings.xml` file with german text.

For example, **/res/values-en/strings.xml** would contain

```
<resources>
    <string name="food">strange meat thing
with weird breadcrumb
    crust</string>
</resources>
```

and **/res/values-de/strings.xml** would contain

```
<resources>
```

```
<string name="food">schnitzel</string>
</resources>
```

Notice that the name attribute to both is common ("food"). When referring to the generated resource id **R.string.food**, if the device's language is set to english, the user will read "strange meat thing with weird breadcrumb crust". If the device's language is set to german, the user will see "schnitzel".

Neat, right?

The Resource Qualifier rabbit hole goes deeper. You can use two or more qualifiers for specific situations: For example, you can show a drawable to Japanese users with -xxxhdpi devices when in landscape orientation by placing your drawable to this a folder called **drawable-jp-land-xxxhdpi/**

Three more things to notice

1. **The order of the qualifiers matters**. In the above example, if I did **drawable-land-jp-xxxhdpi/** (ie. placed land before jp), the folder would be ignored. For the correct order that qualifiers should be put in, go to

https://developer.android.com/guide/topics/resources/providing-resources

2. Always make sure that you have a default, non-qualified version of the **res/** folder you are interested in. For example, if you have a `values-jp/` and a `values-es/` folder (for japanese and spanish respectively), what happens when a user uses a device that has its language set to english? I'll tell you what will happen: the app will crash. So make sure that you also have a plain `values/` folder with the default values that you want to show when one of your more specific cases does not apply.

3. In case it wasn't clear so far, a resource that's meant to be used in different configurations but has the same role within your app should have the exact same filename in different folders with qualifiers. For example, if you have a file called **greek_flag.png** in your `res/drawable-xhdpi` folder, the same icon of a different density in the `res/drawable-xxxhdpi` folder should also be called **greek_flag.png**. Another example: if you have a layout called `activity_main.xml` in the `res/layout-land` folder (that's meant to be displayed when the device is in landscape orientation), the layout for the portrait version of that screen in `res/layout-port` should also be called `activity_main.xml`.

This level of detail is outside the scope of this book, though. Go to

https://developer.android.com/guide/topics/resources/providing-resources to learn more about Resources and qualifiers.

Ok, now that you know how to organize your resources, let's see how you can access them in XML and code.

Accessing resources in XML

Accessing resources in XML is super-easy, barely an inconvenience. Let's say that you have this res/values/strings.xml file

```
<resources>
    <string name="noob_text">Hello
World!</string>
</resources>
```

As you have noticed, the string resource's name is "noob_text". Now, say that you want to place this text in a TextView in a layout of yours. Here is how you can access this resource from the TextView

```
<TextView
```

```
android:layout_width="wrap_content"
android:layout_height="wrap_content"
android:text="@string/noob_text" />
```

See the bolded piece of code? We let the TextView know that we want to refer to a text resource by using the @string part and then after the slash character, we specify which string resource we're referring to.

Just a reminder, since this is supposed to be a beginner book: you may have noticed that I keep adding the `android:layout_width` and `android:layout_height` attributes every time I define a view in XML. Remember: having a view without these attributes will crash you app at runtime!

Want to add some padding to this TextView but don't want to hardcode it in the TextView itself? Ok, let's add a **res/values/dimens.xml** file

```
<resources>
    <dimen
name="hello_world_padding">4dp</dimen>
</resources>
```

Let's add the padding to our TextView

```
<TextView
```

```
android:layout_width="wrap_content"
android:layout_height="wrap_content"
android:text="@string/noob_text"

android:padding="@dimen/hello_world_pad
ding" />
```

Sweet, right? We have referred to a dimension resource by using the @dimen prefix and adding the resource's name after the slash character!

Ready to add some color to this motherfucker?! Let's create a file called res/values/colors.xml

```
<resources>
    <color
name="very_red">#FF0000</color>
</resources>
```

You should be getting the hang of this by now! Let's add the color to our TextView

```
<TextView
    android:layout_width="wrap_content"
    android:layout_height="wrap_content"
    android:text="@string/noob_text"
```

```
android:padding="@dimen/hello_world_pad
ding"
    android:textColor="@color/very_red"
/>
```

So now we've referred to our color resource by using the @color prefix.

Another example, you say? Why, certainly!

Here is an empty ImageView. According to leading ImageViewologists, empty ImageViews wither and die! You wouldn't want this poor ImageView to die, now, *would you, Brian — if that's your REAL name?*

```
<ImageView
    android:layout_width="200dp"
    android:layout_height="200dp"
    android:scaleType="centerCrop" />
```

Let's place an image in this ImageView and save its life! For this, we place the image we want to show in our **res/drawable/** folder. With no qualifiers, for simplicity's sake.

Let's say that the file we placed in our folder is called **monkey.png.** Android will generate a resource id (remember those?) for this image file, called **R.drawable.monkey**. Now we can refer to this image and add it to our ImageView like this

```
<ImageView
    android:layout_width="200dp"
    android:layout_height="200dp"
    android:scaleType="centerCrop"
    android:src="@drawable/monkey"
/>
```

We specify that we want to use a drawable resource by using the @drawable prefix and then add the name of the image file WITH NO EXTENSION!

Accessing resources in Java code

We are finally leaving the markup confines of XML behind us to see how we can refer to our resources using code.

When you add a resource to any of the res/ subfolders (with the exception of /res/assets/), Android creates a resource id for it. I have mentioned resource ids before but *what exactly* are they and where do they come from?

Resource ids are integer values stored in an autogenerated file called **R.java**. The first rule of R.java? *You do not touch R.java.*

Here is an example of an R.java file

```java
public final class R {
    public static final class id {
        public static final int
title_text = 0x7f050000;
        public static final int
subtitle_text = 0x7f050001;
    }
    public static final class drawable {

        public static final int
lightbulb = 0x7f01003d;
```

```
        public static final int scissors
= 0x7f01003e;
    }
    public static final class string {
        public static final int
hello_world = 0x7f010018;
        public static final int
welcome_text = 0x7f010019;
    }
}
```

What the shit is this, right?

I have already mentioned it but it bears repeating: you do not create and you do not touch the R.java file. **The Android build tools generate it for you** and make the necessary changes to it every time it needs to be refreshed.

"So, why are you even showing it to me?" I hear you screaming at the top of your lungs. Well, it's because I want you to understand two things

1. How to access your resources in Java code and

2. Why the type of a resource id is int (integer)

The Android build tools generate the R.java class. Inside the R.java class, it creates static final inner classes and names them after the kind of resource they are. So, an id resource in a TextView like this

```
<TextView
    android:layout_width="wrap_content"
    android:layout_height="wrap_content"
    android:id="@+id/title" />
```

will end up in

```
public final class R {
   public static final class id {
       // ignore the hexadecimal values, I
enter them randomly
       public static final int title =
0x7f010019;
   }
}
```

As you no doubt remember from your Java studies on the Tibetan highlands, referring to a static variable does not require you to instantiate an object of the class (this sounds proper mystical).

So, how do you refer to this resource id in your Java code? Like this

`R.id.title`

Meaning: *in the* `R.java` *class, access the static final class* **id** *and in that class access the static final variable (which, again, is an integer)* `title`.

Easy, right? The exact same thing happens with all resources, so referring to a drawable resource id means doing this

`R.drawable.lightbulb`

When you drag and drop your lightbulb.png file into the /res/drawable/ folder (with or without qualifier), the build tools will generate this

```java
public final class R {
    public static final class drawable {
        public static final int
lightbulb= 0x7f010016;
    }
}
```

Using these resource ids depends on the way you want to use them. Some methods and constructors will take them as an argument, while sometimes you will need to access these resources by using the *.getResources()* method of the Context class.

Here is an example of the former

```
// imageView is an instance of an
ImageView, obvs
imageView.setImageResource(R.drawable.l
ightbulb);
```

In this case, you just pass the resource id to the *.setImageResource(int resourceId)* method of the ImageView class.

Awesome! So that means that, if the TextView class has a `.setText()` method (and it does), I can just go

```
textView.setText(R.string.hello_world);
```

right?

Yes. It will work, in this case. If the only argument you're passing to the `TextView.setText()` method is the string resource id, your text will show normally (because there's an overloaded version of `.setText()` that takes a resource id as an argument).

A Note on Method Overloading

A class can have two or more methods with the same name and return type but different argument lists. The argument lists could differ in number of parameters, order of parameters or type of parameters.

So the TextView class can have two or more setText() methods, as long as the argument lists for these two methods are different.

This is why it's possible to have both a

```
TextView.setText(int resourceID)
```

and a

```
TextView.setText(CharSequence text)
```

method. The methods have the same name but their argument types are different. In fact, the TextView class has even more overloaded .setText() methods with different argument lists, that we will not cover here.

However, sometimes you want to concatenate the text from the string resource with another string. Let's say that you have this `strings.xml` file

```
<resources>
    <string name="hello">Hello,
</string>
</resources>
```

which adds this entry in `R.java`

```
public final class R {

    public static final class string {
        public static final int hello =
0x7f010019;


    }
}
```

You want your app to welcome your user. Your user has already entered his name upon sign-up and he's called "Dave". So you decide to do this

```
// you have already set String userName
equal to the user's username
textView.setText(R.string.hello +
userName);
```

and you expect the user to see "Hello, Dave" displayed on his screen.

What your user will see instead is something like "2130771993Dave". As far as Dave knows, **2130771993** (which is the *decimal* representation of the *hexadecimal* **0x7f010019**) is a swearword in Swahili (yeah, Dave's a dumbass), so he uninstalls the app, gives you a 1-star rating in the Play Store and your career is over. *Over, I tell you!*

What the hell happened here?

You must remember that a static final field in R.java is an **integer**.

TextView's .setText() method can take either an integer or a String as an argument.

If we pass .setText() an integer as an argument, what will happen is that the version of .setText() that takes an integer as an argument will run. Conversely, if we pass it a String as an argument, the version of the method that takes an String as an argument will run.

So passing .setText() the number **2130771993** tells it to go through resources,find the resource with an ID of 2130771993 and set the text it refers to as the TextView's content.

When you pass it the argument **R.string.hello + username,** what you are passing is

```
2130771993 + "Dave"
```

This concatenates the integer with the String and creates a new String that's "2130771993Dave". This new String is then passed to the .setText() method that takes a String as an argument (which will display the literal text it was passed) and the user sees 2130771993Dave on their screen.

Always remember that resource ids are integers.

Now, what can you do about it?

In this case, you have to use the .getResources() method of the Context class and retrieve a **Resources object**. If you're in an Activity (which is a subclass of Context, so you have access to that class's methods), you can do this

```
// get string value from Resources
String hello =
getResources().getString(R.string.hello
);

// concatenate the strings normally
```

```
textView.setText(hello + userName);
```

or in a single statement

```
textView.setText(getResources().getStri
ng(R.string.hello) + userName);
```

Because this type of method chaining might look confusing, let me explain what is happening, step by step

```
// if the class you're currently in is a Context
subclass, call the getResources() method it
inherits from Context
// In this example, we are in an Activity class,
which is a subclass of Context
// so we have access to the getResources method

// step 1: get a Resources object
Resources resources = getResources();

// step 2: use the .getString(int resID) method of
Resources
String hello =
resources.getString(R.string.hello);
// OR SIMPLY chain the methods and do it in one
line
```

```
// step 1, there's no step 2!
String hello =
getResources().getString(R.string.hello);
```

Using the Context.getResources() method, you can retrieve other types of resources, such as dimension resources, eg

```
int height =
getResources().getDimension(R.dimen.but
ton_height);
```

Activities

Getting Java with it: Coding the app

The Activity

Again, let's borrow from the Android docs about what an Activity is

> *An activity is a single, focused thing that the user can do. Almost all activities interact with the user, so the Activity class takes care of creating a window for you in which you can place your UI with* `setContentView(View)`.

Essentially, in the huge majority of cases, an Activity is going to be representing *a screen of your application*. For example, let's say that you have downloaded an app that requires you to sign in. The screen in which you're using your credentials to sign in is quite probably a different screen from the one you're in when you are actually using the app (eg. playing a track or composing an e-mail).

When you want to add an Activity to your application, these are the three things you usually have to do:

1. Create a Java file. This file is going to be called something like, say, NewActivity.java (although more descriptive names are encouraged, like SongDetailsActivity).

2. Create an XML layout file that will contain the layout for that specific activity, for example activity_new.xml

3. Create an entry for the Activity in AndroidManifest.xml. If you don't create an entry for the new activity in AndroidManifest.xml, **your app will crash** when you try to launch the Activity.

When you ask Android Studio to create a new empty Activity for you (*via File -> New -> Activity -> Empty Activity*), it will take care of these steps for you, if you follow the wizard.

The Java file is going to be something like

```
package com.example.noob;
import android.os.Bundle;
public class NewActivity extends
Activity {

    @Override
    protected void onCreate(Bundle
savedInstanceState) {
```

```
super.onCreate(savedInstanceState);

setContentView(R.layout.activity_new);
    }
}
```

Let's forget about the *package name* and *imports* part (it's the same as any other Java source file) and see what's happening here.

First, you will notice that **NewActivity extends Activity**. Since NewActivity is a subclass of Activity, it inherits all of the base class's methods. On the very next line, you see one of these methods being used

```
.onCreate(Bundle savedInstanceState)
```

.onCreate() is the first method called when an Activity is launched.

An Activity instance has a *lifecycle*: when certain things happen (events), certain methods are called. Read this line again and understand it. It's very important.

Another example of a lifecycle event and corresponding callback is the .onPause() method: if the user is in an Activity and, while being in that Activity, decide to press the power button to turn off the screen, the onPause() method is called. In this case, the **event** was the user turning off the screen by pressing the power button. The **lifecycle method** (also known as a callback) triggered when that event happened was the Activity's .onPause() method.

You must have noticed that .onCreate() is passed an argument: an instance of a **Bundle** called savedInstanceState (the name is irrelevant, of course: you could change its name to hugeTastyBurger if you wanted. And I regularly do, for the lolz).

This Bundle object contains information about the Activity's previously frozen state. Let us go on a detour to explain this further.

Scenic Detour: Activities and Configuration Changes

OK. So, you hold your phone in portrait and then you rotate it to landscape. If the app does not block orientation changes (that happens when you specify that your app can only be used in portrait or landscape mode in AndroidManifest.xml*), the Activity will rotate to follow the orientation change.*

When an Activity rotates, a lifecycle method, .onDestroy()*, gets called. There is a way to disable this behaviour, but you really shouldn't.*

*This happens because Android needs to **recreate the Activity**. For example, remember how you can have different folders like* `res/layout-port/` *and* `res/layout-land/` *in your resources folder, each with its own activity_main.xml file? When the device is rotated, if Android is to use the alternate layout file for the alternate configuration (ie. load the landscape version of activity_main.xml when before it was using the portrait version of it), the Activity has to be destroyed and then recreated (ie. call* `.onDestroy()` *and then* `.onCreate()` *again).*

*An orientation change is not the only thing that causes this behaviour. Some events, cumulatively known as **runtime configuration changes**, will destroy and recreate the Activity. Another example of a configuration change at runtime would be a change of device language in the settings.*

Before an Activity is destroyed, a method named `.onSaveInstanceState()` *is called. This method can be overriden and allows you to save the state of the Activity. The Activity will save some view data automatically by using* `super.onSaveInstanceState()` *—the superclass implementation- but for the rest of the Activity state not handled automatically by the system (eg. the user's current position in a ListView), you have to do it yourself.*

*All these changes are saved in a **Bundle** object. A Bundle object is an object that is usually used to pass data between activities. For example, to put a String in a Bundle you'd go*

```
Bundle bundle = new Bundle();
bundle.putString("key", "value");
```

This bundle will be passed to the Activity when `onCreate()` *is called after a configuration change. This is why* `onCreate()` *is passed a Bundle, conventionally called savedInstanceState: to allow it to restore its state after the configuration state.*

If the Activity is just getting created and not recreated, the Bundle object is going to be null.

After the `.onCreate()` declaration, we call `super.onCreate()` and provide it with the Bundle object that was passed to `.onCreate()`. This allows the Activity to automatically take care of its own internal configuration, like attaching a Context to the Activity etc. Doesn't really matter. Learn it by heart. This is how dictatorships rise.

After the call to `super.onCreate()`, we come to the *good stuff.*

On the next line, we see a call to **setContentView()**. This is an Activity method and it lets you pass (among other things) it a resource ID. The resource ID that you pass it should be an XML layout file that is placed in your `res/layout/` folder.

Yep, this is how you display those juicy XML files I showed you how to create earlier in the book on the screen!

setContentView( ) will take the layout and *inflate* it, which means turn it into visible stuff that you see on your screen.

Your basic training is almost complete, young Padawan. At this point, I'd just like to urge to to study the Activity lifecycle early in your Android development career. You don't have to learn it by heart but at least remember:

1. When an Activity is first created (or recreated) **onCreate( )** is called.

2. When an Activity loses focus (eg. a dialog is displayed, the user turns off the screen or presses the home button), **onPause( )** is called.

3. When a configuration change happens or you exit the Activity using the "back" button, **onDestroy( )** is called.

Trust me: I know it sounds complicated right now, but when you reach the point where you're thinking "hm... I want to stop this countdown timer I created when the screen turns off and resume it when the screen turns on", you'll be glad for all the lifecycle callbacks you have available, you ungrateful dog!

Here is a chart from *developer.android.com*. Keep it in mind, hang it on your wall, look at it when you need a refresher and as time goes by, you'll learn to use the lifecycle callbacks without any help.

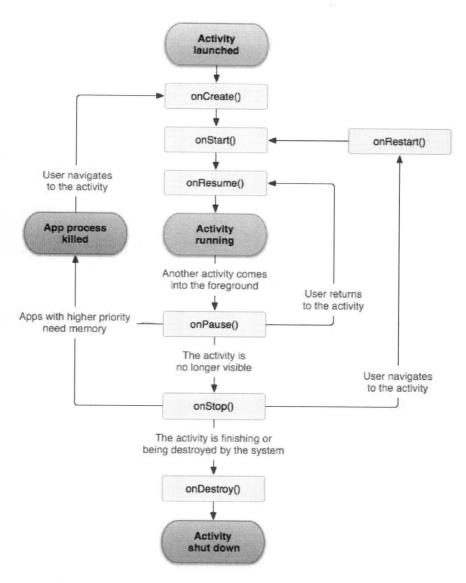

Activity Lifecycle. From developer.android.com. I did not make this. I DID NAHT DO IT! Oh, hi, Mark!

At this point, let's jump into creating a (very simple) app to put those mad skillz you gained to test and start paving the road for your first million-dollar app. Don't worry, it's not going to be a "Hello World!" app.

Interacting with elements in your Activity

Let's start with a simple, but meaningful app. In this app, you'll put a button in the center of your screen. When someone taps this button, a new Activity will be launched. Doesn't sound very impressive but through this simple app, you'll begin to understand a lot of important concepts.

Ok, first let's create a new Android app project in Android Studio. If you don't have Android Studio installed, install it by going to https://developer.android.com/studio/index.html. If the URL has changed in the meantime, Google "Android Studio download" and go to the new download page. When I made a list of the things this book would teach you, I never thought that Google searches would be one of them.

Anyway. Follow the installation instructions for your preferred OS and once you have AS running, come back.

Back for more? Not surprised. Ok, create a new Android app project by going to *File -> New -> New Project*

The next screen is going to ask you to enter the following info

Application name: Enter something descriptive. MyFirstApp sounds fine to me. MyLastApp sounds pretty grim.

Company domain: if you have a domain, eg. www.cucumber.com, enter that. If you don't, just think of one but make it be as unique as you can.

Package name: *the package name has to be unique*, otherwise if you try to upload your app to the Play Store and an app with the same package name exists, you won't be able to publish your app! Android Studio will generate the package name for you, by reversing your domain name and then attaching your app's name at the end. In this case, it'll be com.cucumber.www.myfirstapp (spaces will be removed from your app's name and the characters will all be lowercase).

To continue, select "Next" and on the next page, check "Phone and tablet" and then select a Minimum SDK level. This corresponds to the lowest version of Android your app will be able to run on. At this point (late 2016) I'd suggest that you select API 19 (Kit Kat, yum!).

API 21 (Lollipop) made some sweeping changes to Android but we won't be needing any of that for now. On the next page, select "Empty Activity", click "Next" and on the last page, accept the defaults (the Activity name should be MainActivity, make sure "Generate layout file" is selected and that the Layout name is activity_main).

Wait for Android Studio to spazz out for a bit, especially if you're on an older machine, and then we're all set!

In your editor, you'll see two files: **MainActivity.java** and **activity_main.xml**

Android Studio will immediately go full asshole on us by making me break my promise. In the XML layout file, there will be a TextView saying "Hello World!". Remove that accursed view from the layout by deleting the TextView (click the TextView and press the delete key). Also remove all padding attributes from the root RelativeLayout. You'll be left with this activity_main.xml layout file

```
<?xml version="1.0" encoding="utf-8"?>
<RelativeLayout

xmlns:android="http://schemas.android.com/apk/res/android"

xmlns:tools="http://schemas.android.com/tools"
    android:layout_width="match_parent"
    android:layout_height="match_parent"

tools:context="com.cucumber.www.myfirstapp.MainActivity">
```

```
</RelativeLayout>
```

Cool. We're left with a root RelativeLayout that will take up the entirety of the screen, since both *android:layout_width* and *android:layout_height* are set to "match_parent".

Ready to place something we can tap in the layout? Let's make it a new TextView. In the RelativeLayout, place a TextView and center it in the layout.

There is an *android:layout_**something*** attribute that centers a view in its parent. Try to remember which one it is but if you don't, no sweat. Here we go

```
<?xml version="1.0" encoding="utf-8"?>
<RelativeLayout

xmlns:android="http://schemas.android.com/apk
/res/android"

xmlns:tools="http://schemas.android.com/tools
"
    android:layout_width="match_parent"
    android:layout_height="match_parent"

tools:context="com.cucumber.www.myfirstapp.Ma
inActivity">
```

```
<TextView
    android:id="@+id/tappable_view"
    android:layout_width="wrap_content"
    android:layout_height="wrap_content"
    android:text="TAP ME!"
    android:layout_centerInParent="true"
/>
</RelativeLayout>
```

As you can see, I have given the view an id of "tappable_view". If you run the app now and try to tap the TextView, nothing will happen. The TextView is not yet clickable.

Scenic Detour: Running your app

Speaking of running your app, you have two choices to do that: use an emulator or run it on a physical device. While the built-in emulator has gotten really fast, I'd suggest running the app on a physical device. A physical device will allow you to use multi-touch, among other stuff.

If you don't have an Android device at hand, you have to create and launch an emulator in Android Studio. Go to Tools -> Android -> AVD Manager

AVD Manager has a page called "Your Virtual Devices". Click "Create virtual device" and follow the wizard. You will be prompted to select your desired hardware and system image and then verify them. You can then tap the green "Launch" button and you're good to go. But really: get a physical device.

On a physical device, you have to enable USB debugging if you're to run your app through Android Studio. To do that, go to Settings and then at the "About" section. Find the "Build number" item and tap it seven times in quick succession (that was mildly suggestive). I am not kidding. A pop-up will appear that will say "You are now a developer".

If you go back to the main Settings screen, you will find a new section called "Developer Options". In Developer Options, scroll down until you find an item called Enable USB Debugging and switch that mother on! You can now run your app on the device using the green "Launch" icon in Android Studio.

Keep in mind that these steps may be different, depending on the device you're using. If you are having trouble turning USB Debugging on, Google "[your device] + turn on developer options"

Let's make the TextView clickable. This is going to be amazing. To make something respond to a touch event, you have to set a **listener** on it. A listener is an interface of the View class that contains a single method that fires when that event happens. It's an easy concept to grasp and it'll become even clearer with an example.

First, let's see how we can refer to a View defined in XML in our Java code. For a view to be referable from our Java code, we have to give that view an ID in our XML document. The view's id, in the example above, is "tappable_view".

To get a reference to it, we use the Activity class's **.findViewById()** method

```
TextView textView = (TextView)
findViewById(R.id.tappable_view)
```

One thing to notice is that we have to cast the returned view down to a TextView, since the *.findViewById()* method returns a plain View object. The .findViewById() method

takes the View's resource ID as an argument, so we pass in
`R.id.tappable_view`

Congrats! You now have a reference to your TextView in your
Java code. Let's make the TextView respond to tapping by
setting a listener on it

```
textView.setOnClickListener(new
OnClickListener() {
    public void onClick(View v) {
        // do your magic here!
    }
});
```

I know this looks complicated if you're just starting out, but this
is what happens:

1. We set an OnClickListener on the TextView by using its
   .setOnClickListener() method (you can do this on
   any View). The .setOnClickListener() method takes
   an instance of an OnClickListener interface (actually, an
   instance of an *implementation* of it)

2. The OnClickListener interface is a SAM (**S**ingle **A**bstract
   Method) interface. That means that, when instantiated,
   we have to implement the single method it contains:
   .onClick()

3. In the .onClick() method, we put the code we want to execute when the View is clicked / tapped.

For example, if you add this code in the .onClick() method

```
textView.setOnClickListener(new
OnClickListener() {
    public void onClick(View v) {
        int a = 1;
        int b = 2;
        int c = a + b;
    }
});
```

the code will run. a, b and c will be declared as integers and the system will do the addition, giving c a value of 3. The only problem here is that won't get to see anything because there is no output. Let's talk about that.

Getting some visible output

In this section, I'm going to describe the various ways I use to get some visible output when I'm developing. Getting visible output is a great way to motivate yourself to keep going. Imagine seeing a "3" printed from the code above! That would be neat, right?

First way: use the Android Monitor section in Android Studio

In the default view, after creating a project in Android Studio, you'll see a section called Android Monitor at the bottom of the page. Click on that and select the **logcat** subsection. Now, you'll be able to log messages into the logcat.

To log messages into the logcat, you can use the **android.util.Log** class, which has a variety of static methods that make your life easier. These methods are

Log.e: use this to log errors

Log.i: use this to log useful information in the logcat. You should be using this one most often

Log.v: use this to log verbose messages, ie. lots of stuff

Log.w: the "w" stands for warning, and you use it for logging stuff that are not exactly an error, but are kinda weird

Log.d: use this for debugging. Log values etc.

Log.wtf (not kidding): shit, I don't know. Log, like, you approaching the event horizon of a black hole.

These methods usually take two arguments (they are overloaded methods, so they may take more or less depending on the use case, but I suggest you start by using the ones with these two arguments): first, a tag and second, your message. You can use anything you want as a tag, but I usually use the name of the class I'm in (for example, if I'm inside MainActivity, I'll use "MainActivity" as a tag). This helps you know where the log message is coming from, especially if you're logging lots of stuff. The tag argument should be of type String.

The second argument, which is your message, should also be a String. If you want to log a number (like the integer 3, in the example above), take the hacky shortcut and concatenate it with a String, eg. c + "" or "the value you are logging is " + c.

To log the value of c after the onClick() method is called, we should do this

```
textView.setOnClickListener(new
OnClickListener() {
public void onClick(View v) {
        int a = 1;
        int b = 2;
        int c = a + b;
        Log.i("ExampleActivity", "The value of
c is " + c);
    }

});
```

This will display "The value of c is 3" with a tag of ExampleActivity in the logcat! Congrats, you now know that your code is working!

Second way: change something in your UI (not recommended)

I often use this method, but it's a bad, *bad* habit and I should go stand in the corner for 30 minutes while I reconsider my life choices. Changing something on your UI means that you may ship an app that logs messages meant only for you, which can have security implications. It can also make you look completely unprofessional.

Let's do it anyway!

One way to display a message to yourself in your UI, if for some reason you don't want to look at the logcat (eg you're allergic to logcats — I'll get my coat) is to use the **Toast** class and its static method **.makeText()**

For some reason, the Android team decided to call those short, transient messages that appear on your screen for a short time **toast messages**. A lot of apps use these toast messages to display messages to the user, for example "message sent!" or "photo uploaded" etc.

How would you use it to display c's value (3) in the above example? You'd do this

```
Toast.makeText(ExampleActivity.this, "the
value of c is " + c,
Toast.LENGTH_LONG).show();
```

The static .makeText() method takes three parameters:

1. the current Context (because an Activity is a subclass of Context, we can simply refer to the Activity itself, hence ExampleActivity.this)

2. the message we want to display, which should be a
    String

3. an integer parameter, which specifies for how long the
    message will be visible. This parameter can either have
    a value of Toast.LENGTH_LONG or
    Toast.LENGTH_SHORT

**After creating the message with the .makeText() method, don't
forget to chain the .show() method to actually show the
message! Most beginners will forget this and wonder why the
message isn't being displayed. But not *you*, right?**

Other ways to display messages in your UI would be to set a
TextView to a specific value using its .setText() method, but
again, this is not recommended. Just use the freaking logcat.

Baby's (Second) First Program

Let's make a simple application to expand a little on the concepts we have learned so far! Don't worry, it's going to be really easy for a person of your considerable talents.

In this app, we are going to display a screen with an EditText (ie. a text field for input) and a button. The user will be able to enter their name in the EditText and, upon pressing the button, they will be greeted with a Toast message that will say "Hello, [enter user's name here]"

First, create a new project in Android Studio by following the steps I have described. After the project is created, you will be left with two files that are of interest to us, MainActivity.java and activity_main.xml.

Let's take a look at the activity_main.xml file. Whatever it contains, delete it and let's start from scratch.

```
<?xml version="1.0" encoding="utf-8"?>
<RelativeLayout

xmlns:android="http://schemas.android.com/apk/res/android"
    android:layout_width="match_parent"
```

```
    android:layout_height="match_parent" >
</RelativeLayout>
```

Let's place an EditText in our layout

```
    <?xml version="1.0" encoding="utf-8"?>
    <RelativeLayout

xmlns:android="http://schemas.android.com/apk
/res/android"
        android:layout_width="match_parent"
        android:layout_height="match_parent" >
        <EditText
            android:id="@+id/name_input"
            android:layout_width="match_parent"
            android:layout_height="wrap_content"
            android:hint="enter your name here..."
            android:textColor="#000000"
            android:textSize="14sp"
            android:layout_centerInParent="true"
    />
    </RelativeLayout>
```

First, let's see what's wrong with this EditText element: the *android:hint* attribute is hardcoded as a literal string instead of a reference to a string resource. Remember those?

Secondly, the *android:textColor* attribute is also hardcoded, when it could have also been a color resource. Finally, the *android:textSize* attribute could have also been a dimension resource, instead of again being hardcoded.

The above code will make the EditText as wide as its parent layout (and since the RelativeLayout is the root layout, it'll make it as wide as the screen), as high as the content it displays and will center it in the RelativeLayout (*android:layout_centerInParent="true"*)

If you run your app now, you'll see a text input field sitting in the middle of your screen, waiting patiently for you to do something with it. Enter some text, delete it, go crazy. Unfortunately, there's not much more we can do with it yet.

Let's add a button below the EditText

```
<?xml version="1.0" encoding="utf-8"?>
<RelativeLayout

xmlns:android="http://schemas.android.com/apk
/res/android"
```

```
android:layout_width="match_parent"
android:layout_height="match_parent" >
<EditText
    android:id="@+id/name_input"
    android:layout_width="match_parent"
    android:layout_height="wrap_content"
    android:hint="enter your name here..."
    android:textColor="#000000"
    android:textSize="14sp"
    android:layout_centerInParent="true"
/>

<Button
    android:id="@+id/the_button"
    android:text="click me!"
    android:layout_width="wrap_content"
    android:layout_height="wrap_content"
    android:layout_below="@id/name_input"
    android:layout_centerHorizontal="true"
/>

</RelativeLayout>
```

Things that are interesting about the Button element

1. As you can see, I placed the button below the EditText. Since the EditText is centered in the layout (right now,

it's the middle of the screen, since the RelativeLayout is the root layout), the Button should now be exactly below it, right? And it's going to be. However, **it's also going to be to the left of the screen, since we haven't declared a horizontal placement!** To do this, we also have to specify that we want the Button to be centered horizontally, which we do with `android:layout_centerHorizontal="true"`.

2. It is a button.

We are now done with the XML part of our app. Let's move into the Java code and wire everything up!

To start with, I'd suggest that you create two *class-level variables*, one for the EditText and another one for the Button and then initialize them in `.onCreate()` by using the Activity class's `.findViewById()` method

```
public class MainActivity extends Activity {
    EditText inputField;
    Button okButton;

    public void onCreate(Bundle
savedInstanceState) {
```

```
super.onCreate(savedInstanceState);

setContentView(R.layout.activity_main);
        inputField = (EditText)
findViewById(R.id.name_input);
        okButton = (Button)
findViewById(R.id.the_button);
    }
}
```

Why make them class-level variables and not just declare **and** initialize them in .onCreate()? Because this way, you can access these variables in the entire class and not just .onCreate(). Of course, now you'll also have to remember not to use these variables before they are initialized, otherwise you'll get a Null Pointer Exception.

Let's make the Button clickable

```
public class MainActivity extends Activity {

    EditText inputField;
    Button okButton;

        public void onCreate(Bundle
savedInstanceState) {
```

```
super.onCreate(savedInstanceState);

setContentView(R.layout.activity_main);

        inputField = (EditText)
findViewById(R.id.name_input);
        okButton = (Button)
findViewById(R.id.the_button);
        okButton.setOnClickListener(new
OnClickListener() {
            public void onClick(View v)
{

            }
    });
  }
}
```

Now, let's make something happen when the Button is tapped! Inside the onClick() method, we add the code that'll show the Toast with our message

```java
public class MainActivity extends
Activity {

EditText inputField;
Button okButton;

public void onCreate(Bundle
savedInstanceState) {
   super.onCreate(savedInstanceState);

setContentView(R.layout.activity_main);

   inputField = (EditText)
findViewById(R.id.name_input);
   okButton = (Button)
findViewById(R.id.the_button);

   okButton.setOnClickListener(new
OnClickListener() {
      public void onClick(View v) {
         String name =
inputField.getText().toString();
```

```
Toast.makeText(MainActivity.this,
"Hello, " + name,
Toast.LENGTH_LONG).show();


        }
     });
  }
}
```

If you run the app now, enter your name in the EditText and tap the Button, you'll get a Toast message on your screen saying something like "Hello, Anakin". An optional assignment is making the app say "What a dork! Get a life!" if you actually enter Anakin as your name.

As you can see, to get the name out of the EditText, we used its **.getText()** method, which returns an instance of something called an Editable. We then convert that Editable into a String using its **.toString()** method.

One last thing I'd like you to notice: the first argument in Toast's .makeText() method is the Context. Since an Activity is a subclass of Context, we can pass that in. However, instead of simply passing in "this" to refer to the Activity, we specifically pass in "MainActivity.this". Why is that?

Well, when you create an instance of an OnClickListener, you are creating an anonymous class. *If you use "this" in the OnClickListener's onClick() method, you'll be referring to the OnClickListener instance itself,* not the Activity. That's why you need to specify "MainActivity.this".

How did I know how to create an OnClickListener, get the text out of an EditText and show a Toast message the first time I did it?

I probably did a Google search, which is something you have to get used to doing when coding. A great resource to get info about the Android SDK online is (obviously) the Android Developer docs at https://developer.android.com/index.html, although even simple searches with your specific question will likely bring up solutions and answers on Stack Overflow etc.

Before we proceed, here's a challenge for you: I want you to clear the EditText (remove any text that has been entered into the EditText) when the user turns off their device's screen. When the user turns their screen back on, the EditText must be empty. Here are some tips:

1. EditText has a method called .setText()

2. Remember than an Activity has a lifecycle. A method is called when the Activity loses focus (for example the

screen is turned off). The method you probably want to use is **.onPause()**

That's probably too much help, but go ahead anyway. If you still have any trouble achieving this, add some omega-3 fatty acids to your diet and then drop me a line at <u>sebastian212000@gmail.com</u>

Keep in mind that onPause() is not called only when the screen turns off: any other event that will cause the Activity to lose focus is also going to call onPause() but for the purposes of this simple exercise, you don't have to worry about that.

Launching another Activity and some info on the onBackPressed( ) method

While it is possible to have the entire UI for your app contained within a single Activity (maybe the app is simpler than Forrest Gump. Or you've decided to use Fragments, which is a can of worms I'm *not* opening in this book), you'll most likely want to use two or more Activities to represent different parts of your user interface. One example is having your login / register screen represented by one Activity and your main navigation screen represented by another Activity.

For our example, let's say that we have a MainActivity and another Activity called SoSadThatImNotTheMainActivity.

To launch SoSadThatImNotTheMainActivity from MainActivity, you do the following

```
Intent launchActivityIntent = new
Intent(MainActivity.this,
SoSadThatImNotTheMainActivity.class);
startActivity(launchActivityIntent);
```

Intent? What the hell is an Intent? For that, let me go deeper into this matryoshka doll of a book.

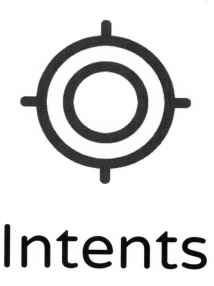

Intents

Intents

Parental Advisory! Explicit Intents!

From the Android docs

> *An intent is an abstract description of an operation to be performed*

Even more helpfully, an Intent is described in another part of the docs as

> *a messaging object you can use to request an action from another app component*

In the last page of the Activity chapter, we used an Intent object to launch an Activity. In this case, we instantiated an Intent object by passing the current Context as the first argument and a Class object (which is the target Activity's Class object) as the second argument. We then launched the target Activity by calling the **startActivity()** method and passing the Intent object as an argument.

The Activity class inherits the `startActivity()` method from the Context class.

This type of Intent is called an **explicit intent**. When we build an explicit intent, *we specify which specific component we want to start* using its fully qualified class name. In this case, it was a specific Activity.

We also use explicit intents to start specific Services. You'll learn more about Services later in this book but, essentially, a Service is a component without a user interface that performs operations in the background. Really stealthily, like a bad motherfucker. *Shhhh, keep your voice down.*

Explicit intents are also used to send broadcasts to Broadcast Receivers. I'll explain later.

OK, so if we have explicit Intents, it makes sense that there should also be **implicit Intents**, correct?

Let me answer that question with a chapter title!

Implicit Intents

When using implicit Intents, we do not name a specific component to be launched. Instead, we declare that **we want an action to be performed** and the systems finds and launches the appropriate component for handling that action.

To make this easier to understand, let's say that you have created a note-taking app. So, in this scenario, your app sucks ass (remember, this is happening in a parallel dimension in which you haven't read this book).

Recognizing the suckiness of your app, you decide to allow users to export what they have already written into another, better app (presumably created by someone who *has* read this book, which has been published in several dimensions).

You can do this by creating an implicit Intent. You set up this Intent to say "Please launch a component that can handle text". The system will go and find a component (usually an Activity) that is capable of importing and handling text and launch it.

All of the above should make you think "Wait. How does the system decide which components are capable of handling a specific type of action? And what happens when there are more than one component capable of handling said action? And, seriously, what do McDonalds put in their chicken nuggets?"

Let's start with the easy part: if you have been using Android for some time, you must have noticed that when you try to share a photo, you get a dialog asking you which app you'd like to use to handle the photo (Gmail, Facebook, Instagram etc). This happens because you have multiple apps capable of handling photos, so Android needs to ask you which app you'd like to use to handle the photo.

This is what happens when you have multiple components capable of handling a specific action: you are offered a choice of apps capable of handling it by the system and you select the one you want to use.

OK, but how does the system know which components are capable of handling this action? This is done through the use of **Intent Filters**.

In your `AndroidManifest.xml` file, you nest an `<intent-filter>` element in the component that you want to handle specific requests. Let's say that you have an `<activity>` element that you want to register as being capable of receiving and handling text (eg. a text editor app). In your manifest file, you do this

```
<activity
android:name="CanAndWillHandleTextActivity">
   <intent-filter>
        <action
android:name="android.intent.action.SEND"/>
        <category
android:name="android.intent.category.DEFAULT
"/>
        <data android:mimeType="text/plain"/>
   </intent-filter>
</activity>
```

As you can see, the <intent-filter> element is nested inside the <activity> element's opening and closing tags. The <intent-filter> element contains three child elements nested inside its opening and closing tags:

which must be set to **android:name="android.intent.category.DEFAULT"** for your activity to even be capable of receiving implicit intents

which specifies that the action to which your activity will respond to is the sending of data (in this specific case)

`<data />` which specifies the kind of data that your activity is capable of handling

This is how the system knows which components are capable of handling specific actions: *the developer declares in the app's manifest* that a specific component of their app is capable of handling a specific kind of action on a specific type of data.

Intent Filters and their **data, action** and **category** tags are a big subject and it's not within the scope of this book to cover every possible combination or use case. However, if you go to https://developer.android.com/reference/android/content/Intent.html, Google's got you covered: you'll find an exhaustive list of available actions, data and categories you can use in your Intent Filters. I almost wrote Intent Fillets. I must be getting hungry.

If you're creating an implicit Intent and want to send some data to the launched component (eg. an Activity that can handle your data), you can do it by attaching your data to the Intent, using its **putExtra()** method.

Attaching data to an Intent, you say?

Passing data between components using Intents

Whether you're using an explicit Intent or an implicit Intent to start an Activity, you can attach data to that Intent that will be passed to the launched Activity.

The way to do this is by attaching your data to your Intent by using its .putExtra() method

```
Intent intent = new Intent(ThisActivity.this,
OtherActivity.class);

intent.putExtra("yourKey", "yourValue");

startActivity(intent);
```

This will launch OtherActivity. To access the data you sent when you're inside OtherActivity, you have to use the getIntent() method, which returns the Intent that started the Activity

```
Intent intent = getIntent();
String data =
intent.getStringExtra("yourKey");
// data will equal "yourValue"
```

While they key should always be a String, the data part doesn't have to be: it can be an integer, a boolean value, an array of booleans etc. You can even pass custom data types that implement either the Serializable or the Parcelable interface but this is a story for another book.

All of this is fine and well when you're starting an Activity using an explicit Intent but how do you send data to another Activity when using an implicit Intent?

Think about it: when you're using an explicit Intent, you control both the sender and the recipient, so to speak. If your key is "myKeyIsSoSick", you'll know that *this* is the key to use when you're trying to retrieve the data in the second Activity.

However, what if you're working on an app that has the ability to import text? Previously, I had shown you how to make your Activity advertise that it can handle text import by adding an Intent Filter to that effect in its Activity element in `AndroidManifest.xml`. Just as a reminder, here is the Intent Filter you'd add in your Activity's tag

```xml
<activity
android:name="CanAndWillHandleTextActivity">
    <intent-filter>
        <action
android:name="android.intent.action.SEND"/>
        <category
android:name="android.intent.category.DEFAULT"/>
        <data android:mimeType="text/plain"/>
```

```
</intent-filter>
    </activity>
```

Now, this Activity is saying to the system "hey, you know what? If an app is sharing (plain) text, show my app in the list of apps capable of handling that text".

The app that's sharing the text is going to be using an implicit Intent to send the text to your app (or any other app capable of handling text). Something like this

```
Intent intent = new
Intent(Intent.ACTION_SEND);
intent.setType("text/plain");
intent.putExtra(Intent.EXTRA_TEXT, "this is
the text I'm sending!");
startActivity(intent);
```

Notice that this Intent object matches the Intent Filter you've added to your Activity's <intent-filter> tag: the data type is set to "text/plain" and the action is defined as ACTION_SEND.

So, how will *your* Activity grab the text and use it? Simple

```
Intent intent = getIntent();
String sentData =
intent.getStringExtra(Intent.EXTRA_TEXT
);
```

```
// sentData will equal "this is the
text I'm sending!"
```

As you can see, the system provides a standardized key of **Intent.EXTRA_TEXT** so that sharing text between activities of different apps using implicit Intents is possible.

While I have focused on sharing text, the Intent class contains other keys you can use to send data to other apps / Activities when using implicit Intents. Here is a great example from the Android developer docs

> For example, when creating an intent to send an email with ACTION_SEND, you can specify the **to** recipient with the EXTRA_EMAIL key, and specify the **subject** with the EXTRA_SUBJECT key.

And that, dear sir or madam, is how you pass and retrieve data between Activities. Well, one of the ways, anyway.

FIRST AND ONLY SUMMARY YOU'LL EVER SEE IN THIS BOOK

Ok, that was a huge information dump. If the rest of the chapters were the result of a human taking a dump, this one was King Kong spraying his mega-shits everywhere (more on King Kong and mega-shits in a bit) .

Let's summarize:

You mostly use Intents to launch Activities and Services.

When using an Intent to launch an Activity, you can either use an implicit or an explicit Intent.

Explicit intents are easy. You only need to specify the Activity you're currently in and the Activity you want to launch

```
Intent intent = new
Intent(CurrentActivity.this,
OtherActivity.class);
```

Sending data from one Activity to the other is also easy. Simply use the `.putExtra()` method, specify a key and a value and retrieve the data from the launched Activity by calling `.getIntent()` and then calling, for example, `.getStringExtra()` (or any other method, like `.getIntExtra()`, depending on the type of data you've attached to the Intent) and passing the key as an argument.

Activity 1 (CurrentActivity)

```
Intent intent = new
Intent(CurrentActivity.this,
OtherActivity.class);
intent.putExtra("name", "Brian Wilson");
startActivity(intent);
```

Activity 2 (OtherActivity)

```
Intent intent = getIntent();
String composerName =
intent.getStringExtra("name");
// composerName equals "Brian Wilson"
```

Things get a bit trickier when using implicit Intents, but not that much trickier.

If you want to **ask for a specific action to be performed**, you need to specify the action you want (eg. ACTION_SEND if you want to send data to the launched Activity or ACTION_CALL if you want your app to use a dialer app to make a phone call) when constructing your implicit Intent. You then add the type of data that you want to send (if applicable) and start the Activity (whichever that will be) by calling startActivity() and passing the Intent as an argument as always.

If you want your Activity to register itself as **being able to carry out a specific action**, you have to add a nested `<intent-filter>` element in your `<activity>`'s element in `AndroidManifest.xml`. That intent filter element must contain the kind of action your Activity is able to perform and on what sort of data it can perform that action on. When other apps send out implicit Intents asking for apps (Activities) that can perform a specific task, if the Intent they send match you Intent Filter(s), your Activity will pop up as being able to handle that action.

Implicit Intents are a bit more complicated to deal with and may require you to go through the documentation (or Stack Overflow) but you should easily be able to do what you want to do after some minor research.

And another thing: startActivityForResult()

I won't go too deep into this but it's interesting to note that you're not limited to simply starting another Activity from the one you're currently in.

You can also start another Activity (which may not be you own app's Activity at all) and get a result from that Activity *back* to your own Activity. As an example, you may want to start a camera Activity to capture a photo and then use that photo within your own Activity.

Other use cases include starting a Contacts app to get a contact's details back to your own app or starting a gallery app to pick an image from there and return it to your own app. You can even use this as a mechanism to retrieve results from your own Activities.

Getting deeper into this is not within the scope of this book so I'll just go have some Cheetos instead. Just keep in mind that it is possible and that it can save you a considerable amount of time, since you can piggyback on the capabilities and user interface of other apps to get data that you need for your own app. Not having to create your own camera app to simply capture a photo is an amazing thing, trust me.

SCENIC DETOUR: King Kong taking a dump

Ok, this may be an Android development book for beginners but don't you ever wonder how King Kong's digestive tract works?

You don't? Really? Weirdo.

I know that King Kong is a fictional character (although women and skyscrapers exist, so why wouldn't King Kong — but I digress) but I make the claim that if King Kong did exist, he wouldn't be able to take a shit. Or at least, his "shit" would look nothing like ours.

How so, you ask? Well, for excrement to be formed from food, intestinal bacteria have to process it in the large intestine. But here's the thing: are those bacteria going to be proportionally large to the size of King Kong?

Of course not. Because then they wouldn't be bacteria — they would be large, slimy balls of goo.

So if the bacteria in King Kong's large intestine are as large as the bacteria in our digestive tract and King Kong has a large intestine with a diameter of a meter or so (rough guess, the films don't mention the exact size), that means that those bacteria won't be able to break down the incoming mass of half-digested leaves, mega-bananas, helicopters and movie villains in time to form what we consider to be excrement.

That is, unless King Kong takes a dump once a month to allow for the mass to be sufficiently broken down. But by then, he'd be farting the entire time because of the gas formed in his intestine during the digestive phase. Have you ever heard King Kong ripping one out? Didn't think so.

Which leads me to conclude that King Kong has regular bowel movements and that most of the food he eats comes out of his asshole almost exactly as it went in.
In conclusion, my comparison of the info dump in the Intents chapter to "King Kong mega-shits" may be flawed but I at least got the chance to write a page about something that has been bothering me since I was a kid.

It was therapeutic. Thanks for reading.

Shared Preferences

Shared Preferences: saving data locally like a boss

There are various ways to save data locally on Android:

1. the SQLite database

2. saving files in the internal or external storage

3. saving key-value sets using the Shared Preferences API.

We'll be discussing Shared Preferences since, in my opinion, its the simplest way to locally save data provided by the Android framework.

Saving data in Shared Preferences essentially means that you'll be saving key-value sets in an XML format. That may sound confusing, but the Shared Preferences API (or SharedPrefs, as its friends like to call it) abstracts that all away for you.

Saving data in SharedPrefs (yeah, we're pals — I've known SharedPrefs longer than I have known my wife) starts with you specifying a file that'll contain the key-value pairs you wish to save.

The Context class has a method called .getSharedPreferences(), which lets you get a reference to a SharedPrefs object. If you're in a class that's a subclass of Context (like an Activity or a Service), you can simply do this

```
SharedPreferences sharedPrefs =
getSharedPreferences("filename", 0);
```

Eagle-eyed readers (or, let's be honest here: not completely dumbass readers) will have noticed that you don't only have to specify a filename. There's a second argument there: an integer. That's the *mode* of the SharedPrefs object to be created. What does that mean?

Passing in 0 (zero) like I did in the example means that the file that'll be created to hold your key-value sets will only be readable and writable from your own application, which is pretty awesome.

The zero actually corresponds to the value of a constant in the Context class called MODE_PRIVATE, which tells you all you need to know. Which means that I could have written the above line as

```
SharedPreferences sharedPrefs =
getSharedPreferences("filename",
Context.MODE_PRIVATE);
```

which, you must admit, is clearer in purpose.

Android Development For Gifted Primates

Cool! File created. Now how do you write in it?

To do that, you have to create another object called an **Editor.**
Editor is actually an inner class of SharedPreferences, so to
obtain a reference to it you do the following

```
SharedPreferences sharedPrefs =
getSharedPreferences("filename",
Context.MODE_PRIVATE);
SharedPreferences.Editor editor =
sharedPrefs.edit();
```

Once you have an Editor object, you can start writing your
key-value pairs. You cannot put simply anything in
SharedPrefs, though. The Editor object has a variety of methods
that only let you enter specific types of primitive values and
objects. In fact, the methods are named after the type they allow
you to store. That's why you have methods named

```
editor.putString()
editor.putBoolean()
editor.putInt()
editor.putFloat()
editor.putLong()
```

All of these methods take a String as a key (ie, the first argument) and a second argument, which is the actual value you want to save.

Let's see how this works in real life with an example. In this very interesting scenario, you have an EditText and a Button on screen. The user must enter their name in the EditText and press the Button. After the user presses the Button, their name will be saved.

But here comes the *good* part: When the user leaves and reenters the app, they will be greeted with their name. If you are a normal, self-respecting person, you'll probably print out something like "Hey, Dave" to them. If you are a juvenile jackass like me, you'll probably say something like "Let me ask your *mom*, Dave!"

First, **activity_mom.xml**

```
<?xml version="1.0" encoding="utf-8"?>
<RelativeLayout

xmlns:android="http://schemas.android.com/apk
/res/android"
    android:layout_width="match_parent"
    android:layout_height="match_parent">
    <TextView android:id="@+id/greeting"
```

```
        android:layout_width="wrap_content"
        android:layout_height="wrap_content"
        android:textSize="14sp"
        android:textColor="#000000"
        android:layout_alignParentTop="true"
/>
    <EditText
        android:hint="enter your name..."
        android:id="@+id/name_field"
        android:layout_width="match_parent"
        android:layout_height="wrap_content"
        android:textSize="14sp"
        android:textColor="#000000"
        android:layout_centerInParent="true"
/>
    <Button android:id="@+id/name_button"
        android:layout_width="wrap_content"
        android:layout_height="wrap_content"
        android:textSize="14sp"
        android:textColor="#000000"
        android:layout_below="@id/name_field"

android:layout_centerHorizontal="true"
        android:text="PRESS ME!" />
</RelativeLayout>
```

And now, for *MomActivity.java*

```java
public class MomActivity extends Activity {

    SharedPreferences sharedPrefs;
    SharedPreferences.Editor editor;
    TextView greeting;
    EditText nameField;
    Button nameButton;
    public static final String USERNAME_KEY =
"username";

    @Override
    protected void onCreate(Bundle savedInstanceState) {
        super.onCreate(savedInstanceState);
        setContentView(R.layout.activity_mom);
        sharedPrefs =
getSharedPreferences("preferences",
        Context.MODE_PRIVATE);
        editor = sharedPrefs.edit();
        greeting = (TextView)
findViewById(R.id.greeting);
        nameField = (EditText)
findViewById(R.id.name_field);
        nameButton = (Button)
findViewById(R.id.name_button);
```

```
        if (sharedPrefs.getString(USERNAME_KEY,
"").isEmpty()) {
            greeting.setVisibility(View.GONE);
        } else {
            String name =
sharedPrefs.getString(USERNAME_KEY, "");
            greeting.setText("Let me ask your mom, " +
name);
        }


        nameButton.setOnClickListener(new
View.OnClickListener() {
            @Override
            public void onClick(View v) {
                if
(nameField.getText().toString().isEmpty()) {
                    Toast.makeText(MomActivity.this,
"Please enter a name, you
                    doofus", Toast.LENGTH_LONG).show();
                } else {
                    String nameToSave =
nameField.getText().toString();
                    editor.putString(USERNAME_KEY,
nameToSave).apply();
                }
            }
        });
```

```
    }
}
```

I have bolded all the interesting lines, so let's go through them together.

```
        SharedPreferences sharedPrefs;
        SharedPreferences.Editor editor;
```

Here, I am declaring the variables, obvs.

```
        public static final String USERNAME_KEY
        = "username";
```

Now, this is nothing special: I am just declaring a constant called USERNAME_KEY, which has a value of "username". I do this to keep the code readable.

```
        sharedPrefs =
        getSharedPreferences("preferences",
        Context.MODE_PRIVATE);
```

This is the cool part: I am getting a reference to a SharedPreferences object by using Context's .getSharedPreferences() method that I mentioned earlier.

Again, take a look at the passed arguments. The first argument is the name of the file that'll contain the saved data (in this case it's "preferences") and the second argument the mode of the SharedPreferences object. In this case, it's MODE_PRIVATE, which means that only our application will be able to read and write to this file.

```
editor = sharedPrefs.edit();
```

We are now getting a handle to a SharedPreferences.Editor object. This object will allow us to write data in the SharedPreferences file.

```
if (sharedPrefs.getString(USERNAME_KEY,
"").isEmpty()) {

greeting.setVisibility(View.GONE);
        }
```

Nice! This is us retrieving data from SharedPreferences. What data, you say? *Exactly!* We haven't written any data using our SharedPreferences.Editor object yet because this is our first time running the app. *We* know that but the app doesn't know it, so we check to see if the user has entered a name. Let's drill down further into this: first we run

```
sharedPrefs.getString(USERNAME_KEY, "")
```

This line uses the SharedPreferences object's .getString() method. Since we have decided that the username is going to be saved as a String (of course it's going to be a String — what is this, *The Prisoner*?) we try to retrieve the name.

As you would imagine, we do this by passing in the key, expecting to be returned the value. OK, why isn't it just

```
// this will not work! lol
sharedPrefs.getString(USERNAME_KEY)
```

then? What is that second empty String argument?
The second argument is **the default value to be returned if there is no value that corresponds to the passed key**.

At this point, since the user hasn't entered a username yet, there is no value saved with a key of USERNAME_KEY. In this case, the default value will be returned, which we have decided to be an empty String (""). We could have called this anything, as long as it's of the correct type (a String, since we are using the .getString() method)

This means that if we use the SharedPreferences.getBoolean() method, the second argument (the default value) should be a boolean value, eg

```
boolean isAwesome =
sharedPrefs.getBoolean(AWESOME_KEY,
false);
```

Back to our line

```
if (sharedPrefs.getString(USERNAME_KEY,
"").isEmpty()) {

    greeting.setVisibility(View.GONE);
        }
```

After retrieving the value associated with USERNAME_KEY, we use the String class's .isEmpty() method to see if what's returned is an empty String. When the program runs for the first time, it actually *is* an empty String (**our default value**) since no username has been saved yet. So we go ahead and use the .setVisibility() method of the View class to change the visibility of the greeting TextView into Gone (the View disappears from the screen and stops taking up any space).

A quick note: View.setVisibility() can be passed three different values

1. **View.GONE**: The View disappears from the screen and any space allocated to it is gone with it

2. **View.INVISIBLE**: The view becomes invisible but any space allocated to it remains on screen as empty space

3. **View.VISIBLE**: the View remains (or becomes, if it was previously hidden or gone) visible

```
else {
        String name =
sharedPrefs.getString(USERNAME_KEY, "");
        greeting.setText("Let me ask your
mom, " + name);
    }
```

This code block runs if a username has already been entered by the user. Since the default value returned in our if-statement above wasn't an empty String, that means that some sort of username has been entered into SharedPreferences with a key of USERNAME_KEY.

We retrieve it by using the .getString() method again and greet the user. OK, make fun of the user's mom. Tomato, tomahto.

```
nameButton.setOnClickListener(new
View.OnClickListener() {
        @Override
        public void onClick(View v) {
```

```
                          if
            (nameField.getText().toString().is
            Empty()) {

        Toast.makeText(MomActivity.this, "Please
        enter
                          a name, you doofus",
                          Toast.LENGTH_LONG).show();

                      } else {

                          String nameToSave =
                                nameField.getText
                          ().toString();

                          editor.putString(USERNA
                          ME_KEY, nameToSave).apply();
                      }
                  }
            });
```

Here, we set an OnClickListener to the Button. When the button is tapped, first we check to see if the user has actually entered a name or if the EditText is still empty (notice that we use the very handy .isEmpty() method of the String class again to check that). If it is empty, we kindly remind the user to enter a username.

The interesting part happens when the user actually enters something in the text field.

```
String nameToSave =
nameField.getText().toString();
editor.putString(USERNAME_KEY,
nameToSave).apply();
```

First we extract the name from the EditText. Then we save the String into SharedPreferences by using the editor's .putString() method. This method takes the **key as its first argument** (always a String, even when using its sibling methods .putBoolean(), .putLong() etc) and **the value we want to save as its second argument** (in this case, a String with the text the user has entered).

See that chained `.apply()` method? **<u>NEVER FORGET</u>** to call .apply() when you have put a value into SharedPreferences using the Editor. **If you don't call .apply(), your changes WON'T BE SAVED!**

Instead of .apply(), you can also call .commit().

The difference? `.apply()` does not return any value and its asynchronous.

`.commit()` returns true if the write operation was successful and false if the write operation failed.

Just use `.apply()`!

The end? Yep. Kind of. If you want, start going through the code again but this time think about what will happen if this is the second run and the user has entered a username.

A couple more things about the Editor

If you want to remove a value from SharedPreferences, just call the Editor's `.remove()` method and pass it the key of the value you want to remove. In our previous example, you'd remove the username from SharedPreferences by doing

```
editor.remove(USERNAME_KEY).apply();
```

See that `.apply()` call? Good.

If you want to delete everything from SharedPreferences, just use the Editor's `.clear()` method

```
editor.clear().apply();
```

See that `.apply()` call that I *accidentally* bolded? You get the point.

Services

Services

Like Activities, Services are one of the main components of Android.

Unlike Activities, though, Services don't have a user interface. Services are meant to perform long-running background operations. Stuff like downloading files in the background or playing music while you're browsing the interwebs are implemented using Services.

Similarly to Activities, Services can be started by using the `.startService()` method of the Context class.

This is how you start a Service called MyService, for example

```
Intent intent = new Intent(MainActivity.this,
MyService.class);
startService(intent);
```

Pretty easy, right?

Another similarity Services have to Activities is the fact that **they have to be declared in your app's `AndroidManifest.xml` file.** If you don't declare them in your manifest but try to start them, *nothing will happen.*

Contrary to what happens with Activities that haven't been declared in the manifest (which crash when you try to start them), undeclared Services will simply not run. What the fuck is that all about?

A Story from the Trenches

I remember back in 1915, during World War I, being in the trenches and trying to figure out why my Service subclass wouldn't run. As if that wasn't enough, those damn Krauts were bombing my ass the entire time, causing mud to land on the screen of my touchscreen laptop and completely by accident opening porn sites in the browser I was using for research.

It took me until the start of the Great Depression to realize that I hadn't declared my Service subclass in the manifest, at which point I was in such a terrible financial state I had to sell my laptop to a Polish dentist in New York simply to use his toilet. But boy, did I use that toilet.

Anyway, enough reminiscing.

Types of Services

On Android, there are two types of Services

1. **Started services**: this type of Service is launched by another Android component, such as an Activity. Started services can communicate with the component that has launched them by using Intents or callbacks. However, for situations where frequent communication with other components is required, you're better off using the second type of Service

2. **Bound services:** A bound Service is, as the Android docs nicely put it, the server in a server-client interface. Bound services allow other app components to bind to them (hence the name) and interact with them in a more elegant way than a started Service would allow.

We are not going to be looking into bound services in this book since (believe me) they are not the domain of the novice Android programmer. Hell, mention AIDL to even experienced Android developers and watch them quiver.

Started services are easier to deal with. To create a Service, you first have to extend the Service class and then implement the **.onStartCommand( )** and **.onBind( )** methods.

```java
public class SomeService extends Service {

    public SomeService() {
    }
    @Override
    public int onStartCommand(Intent intent,
int flags, int startId) {

        // wooo! look at me doing useful
    things!

        return Service.START_NOT_STICKY;
    }
    @Override
    public IBinder onBind(Intent intent) {
        // not a bound service, so we return
    null
        return null;
    }
}
```

Don't forget to declare the Service in `AndroidManifest.xml`

```xml
<service
        android:name=".SomeService"
```

```
android:enabled="true"
    >
</service>
```

`.onStartCommand()` passes an Intent as its first argument, which is the Intent that started the Service. Through that Intent, you can pass data to the Service from the component that started it. If, for example, you want to download a file from a URL, you can pass a String of the URL from the Activity that started the Service and then use that URL in the Service itself to download the file.

You may have noticed that `.onStartCommand()` returns an integer. In this case, it's a constant in the Service class called `START_NOT_STICKY`. There are other return values, like `START_STICKY` and `START_REDELIVER_INTENT` and they are related to the Service's lifecycle.

Stopping a Service

To stop a started Service, all you have to do is call `Service.stopSelf()` from within the Service itself or call `Context.stopService()` from the component that has launched the Service.

When calling `Context.stopService()` from the component that has launched the Service (eg. an Activity), you have to pass the Intent you have used to start the Service as an argument to `.stopService()` like this

```
Intent intent = new Intent(MainActivity.this,
SomeService.class);
startService(intent);
// some time later, porn has been downloaded
stopService(intent);
```

In which thread does a Service run?

It may surprise you to learn that, for all the talk about how a Service is meant to perform long-running tasks in the background, *it does not run on its own thread by default. **It runs on the UI thread.***

This means that if you start a Service and try to perform a long-running task in the `.onStartCommand()` method, you'll make your app hang and eventually crash and burn.
The solution? In `.onStartCommand()`, start your own thread and perform the long-running task in there.

IntentService

All of this stuff sounds like a bit of a hassle, doesn't it?

You have to start the Service, take care of the threading yourself and then stop the Service when it has performed its task.

I mean, don't get me wrong: Services are cool. They allow us to do cool stuff that wouldn't be possible otherwise. To me, Services are like that old, kind but sort of stuffy butler in a period drama. Or the sweet, grandmotherly maid that bakes some awesome muffins but also moves your stuff around and puts it where "it should be". Useful, but also a bit annoying.

But IntentService? Oh, man, IntentService.

Old, kind and stuffy butler? Forget about that shit! How about a ripped poolboy than can also mix you a mean cosmo? Sweet, grandmotherly maid? Yeah, right. How about a hot nurse-maid hybrid in satin and lace? That's IntentService.

Why do I like the IntentService class so much? Well, this is why: once you've started an IntentService, *it runs on its own thread* (so no UI blocking and no need to create a thread yourself) and *it stops itself once its task is finished.* So you don't have to.

So, no drawbacks?

IntentService is actually just a subclass of Service, with most of the complexity taken care of for you. This also means that an IntentService is less flexible than a plain old started, non-Intent Service.

Since it stops itself when its task is finished means that it is not very useful in some specific cases, such as when making a music player app. Moreover, interfacing and interacting with it is more of a hassle, since it's a started and not a bound service.

Finally, an IntentService puts requests to it in a queue and can't perform those requests concurrently, which is something easy to do with a plain started Service.

For a developer that's just starting out, however, an Intent Service should be able to cover a lot of common scenarios.

An example of an IntentService

Let's see how we can start an Intent Service and download some stuff from a URL. The networking part is not the point, but it'll give you a glimpse into HttpUrlConnection, which you can use to connect to the internet.

I personally use Retrofit (a networking library by Square) for networking and I suggest that you do the same when you reach the point that you have to connect to a server or use an API.

```
public class AnActivity extends
Activity {
    public void onCreate(Bundle
savedInstanceState) {

super.onCreate(savedInstanceState);

setContentView(R.layout.some_xml_file);
        String url =
"http://www.google.com";
        Intent intent = new
Intent(AnActivity.this,
MyIntentService.class);
        intent.putExtra("url", url);
        startService(intent);
    }
}
```

Just as we do when trying to launch an Activity, we construct an Intent with two parameters: the current Context (MainActivity.this) and a Class object that represents the Service we are going to launch.

We then put a String extra in the Intent, which is the URL we are going to be connecting to in IntentService and launch the Service by passing the Intent object to the `.startService()` method of the Context class (remember, Activity is a subclass of Context, so the method is available to Activities).

This will launch MyIntentService, which is this

```java
public class MyIntentService extends
IntentService {

// interesting part 1: you have to create a
default constructor
// and call the super implementation and
pass a String to it

    public MyIntentService() {
        super("MyIntentService");
    }

    @Override
    protected void onHandleIntent(Intent
intent) {



    }
```

```
        }
```

The two things you definitely have to do is

1. create a default no-argument constructor and call the
    super implementation. Then pass the .super() call a
    String that identifies your Service. Any String will do, it
    doesn't have to be the class's name.

2. implement .onHandleIntent() and do your work in
    that method.

See that Intent object that's passed to us as an argument to
.onHandleIntent()?

Yep: that's the actual Intent that we used to start the
IntentService back in AnActivity. Which means that you can
now extract the String we sent from AnActivity to
MyIntentService. The key of the extra we attached to the Intent
was "url", so we'll use that to retrieve the URL String

```
public class MyIntentService extends IntentService
{

        public MyIntentService() {
                super("MyIntentService");
```

```
    }

    @Override
    protected void onHandleIntent(Intent intent)
{

        String url =
intent.getStringExtra("url");
    // what follows is a bit of networking logic to
connect to the
        URL. Not the point, but follow along if you
want

        try {
// convert String to an actual URL object
                URL actualUrl = new
URL(url);
// create a new HttpUrlConnection object, which
allows the
// connection to the network
                HttpURLConnection connection =
(HttpURLConnection) url.openConnection();
// request a connection to the URL
                connection.connect();

// get an input stream from the URL we have
connected to
```

```
            InputStream inputStream =
connection.getInputStream();


// create an input stream reader, feed it the
input stream and an
// the desired encoding (utf-8 in this case)

            InputStreamReader isReader = new
InputStreamReader(inputStream, "UTF-8");
// wrap a buffered reader around the input stream
reader to make the operation more efficient

            BufferedReader bufferedReader =
new BufferedReader(isReader);

            String finalPage = "";
            String appendedData = "";
// iterate through the lines of the buffered
reader until there are no lines left and construct
the final HTML string by concatenating the lines
together
        while ((appendedData =
        bufferedReader.readLine()) != null){
                finalPage += appendedData +
"\n";
        }
```

```
        }


    catch (Exception e) {
        // break every exception-handling rule in
the book by catching a base Exception and get f-ed
in the a- by experienced Java developers or Reddit
know-it-alls


        }


    }
}
```

As I said, the networking code is not important (and you should be using Retrofit anyway) but I added some comments so you can follow along if you want!

The important part is that, since this is an IntentService, **the service itself will do the network operation in its own worker thread.**

This is really important, because doing such an operation on the main thread (as a plain ol' Service would do, without you creating the thread yourself) **will cause your app to stop responding while the operation is being performed**. In fact, Android will NOT let you do a network operation on the main thread and will instead throw an exception.

However, there are other long-running operations that Android *will* allow on the main thread, causing your app to (in ascending order of fuckshittiness) lag, momentarily hang, become unresponsive, throw an ANR (application not responding) error, cause a rip in the fabric of time and space or play the Celine Dion song from Titanic.

See how cool IntentService is?

Anyway! Want to do one last VERY cool thing as a bonus? Want to show the user a notification in the status bar when the page has finished downloading?

Oh, I bet you do!

Notifications

Bonus awesome: NotificationManager, Notification and Notification.Builder

Creating and showing notifications

I wasn't going to include a section about Notifications in this book at all but I decided to go ahead and include a bonus mini-chapter about it since

1. It's really quite simple to do.

2. I will get to show you a pattern that's used very often in Android development

Notifications are used to let the user know that something that's worth being notified about has happened. SMS and instant messaging notifications are a very good example of this. Spammy notification from games are a really bad example of this.

Notifications appear in what's called notification tray, shade or drop-down. It's what you pull down from the top of the screen to access your notifications. If you don't pull the notification shade down, you can still see the icons for the notifications you have in your status bar.

To show a notification, we start by retrieving a system service called Notification Manager. We do this by using the `.getSystemService()` method of the Context class.

```
NotificationManager notificationManager =
(NotificationManager)
getSystemService(Context.NOTIFICATION_SERVICE
);
```

Before we continue to create and show our notification, a note on system services.

Accessing system services

This is a pattern that's used very often in Android development. Retrieving a system service using `.getSystemService()` lets you access other important parts of the Android framework like

- the **AlarmManager** (to create repeating tasks)
- the **DownloadManager** (to deal with HTTP downloads easily)
- the **LocationManager** (for dealing with location-related functionality)
- the **LayoutInflater** (for inflating XML layouts) and
- the **Vibrator** (I kid you not) to deal with the vibration hardware

As with the NotificationManager, to retrieve these system services you have to use `.getSystemService()` and pass it a constant from the Context class. To access the aforementioned services you have to pass these constants

- for AlarmManager, you have to call .getSystemService(**Context.ALARM_SERVICE**)
- for DownloadManager, call .getSystemService(**Context.DOWNLOAD_SERVICE**)
- for LocationManager, call .getSystemService(**Context.LOCATION_SERVICE**)
- for LayoutInflater, call .getSystemService(**Context.LAYOUT_INFLATER_SERVICE**)
- for Vibrator, call 800-SEX-ROBOT. Sorry, it was too easy. Call .getSystemService(**Context.VIBRATOR_SERVICE**)

Remember to always cast to the type of Service you retrieve, since `.getSystemService()` returns an Object object.

Now that you have a NotificationManager, you have to construct a Notification object using Notification.Builder

```
Notification notification = new
Notification.Builder().setContentTitle(
"title").
```

```
setContentText("text").setSmallIcon(R.d
rawable.notification_icon).build();
```

To create the Notification object, you first create a Notification.Builder and then chain (setter) method calls to customize your Notification just the way you want it.

Calling **.setSmallIcon()**, **.setContentText()** and **.setContentTitle()** is <u>mandatory</u>. You cannot build a Notification that does not contain these three important pieces of info.

You can then proceed to set other properties of the Notification as required but *always make sure that these three methods are called before building the Notification.*

Then call .build() and your Notification is ready!

But just because it's built does not mean that it's shown to the user: you now have to use the .notify() method of the NotificationManager object to actually display the Notification.

```
int notifId = 1;
notificationManager.notify(notifId,
notification);
```

The first argument of the `.notify()` method is an integer that's the unique notification id. This is up to you to specify and it's the same id you'll have to use to dismiss the notification using the NotificationManager's `.cancel()` method.

So, if any reason you want to dismiss the notification, all you have to do is

```
notificationManager.cancel(notifId);
```

and the Notification will disappear.

In our IntentService example, let's take a look at the code we'll have to add so that a notification will be shown to the user, letting them know that the webpage has been downloaded

```
int notificationId = 1;

NotificationManager notificationManager =
(NotificationManager)

getSystemService(Context.NOTIFICATION_SERVICE
);

Notification notification = new
Notification.Builder().setSmallIcon(R.drawabl
e.icon).setContentTitle("Download
```

```
finished!").setContentText("The webpage has
been downloaded successfully").build();

notification.notify(notificationId,
notification);
```

In the last two chapters we started an IntentService, downloaded a webpage and notified the user that the webpage has been downloaded. I also took a huge dump while you weren't looking.

But there's still something missing. Wouldn't it be awesome if there was a way to send the downloaded webpage back to the Activity that started the IntentService?

Turns out, there is! And you'll learn how to do just that in our final chapter, Broadcast Receivers & You.

Broadcast Receivers

Broadcast Receivers & You

Welcome to the final chapter of this book. If you've made it this far, give yourself a pat on the back.

Just kidding. It's a thirty thousand words-long book. Even my grandma could do it, if she wasn't busy knitting. Knowing how to knit: now *that* deserves a pat on the back.

Early in the planning of this book (yes, there was actual planning involved) I decided to cover Broadcast Receivers last, since you have to already have a good understanding of the other components of Android (especially Activities and the Intent system) to really get what they are about.

When I was starting out, I struggled to really get what Broadcast Receivers were about and what they were useful for. Since then, I've developed an ingenious way of conceptualizing them in real-life terms, and you can learn all about it by signing up for my Broadcast Receiver masterclass for only $250 US for a limited time.

PSYCH! I'll tell you all about it here.

Radio Days: an analogy about Broadcast Receivers

If you've ever used an FM radio (which is increasingly unlikely in these days of Spotify and music-on-demand everywhere) you'll know how that you have to tune your device (the radio) to a specific frequency (eg. 99.4 FM) to listen to a specific radio station.

Broadcast Receivers can be easily understood if you think about them in terms of radio signals.

What's the first thing that has to happen for you to listen to a radio station? Something has to *transmit a signal*.

Android transmits a signal by using the .sendBroadcast() method of the Context class.

What does a radio signal carry? Data, of course. I won't get into the specifics here, partly because that would be tedious and partly because I have no clue how frequency modulation or amplitude modulation work but your favorite All 4 One songs are converted in transmittable data and then transmitted.

In Android, data is carried by an Intent object. When you call the .sendBroadcast() method, you supply it with an Intent that contains the data you want to transmit. Remember those

`.putExtra()` methods? Put them to good use here by loading your Intent with data that will be carried somewhere.

Alright. So now you've used the `.sendBroadcast()` method as your transmitter and the Intent object as the data your transmission carries. What is the receiver, in this analogy? What if I told you that it's called a (PLOT TWIST) Broadcast Receiver?

To create a Broadcast Receiver, you subclass the BroadcastReceiver class and override its `.onReceive()` method. There are actually two types of Broadcast Receivers, **Context-registered** ones and **Manifest-registered** ones. More info on these later.

In our radio analogy, how do you tune into a broadcast? Obviously, just like in radio transmissions, there are going to be a lot of transmissions going on at a given time but you only choose to listen to a specific station by tuning into it.

In Android, you tune into a specific frequency by using an Intent Filter. This will (literally) filter all broadcasts and tune into the one your Receiver is listening to.

Once your Receiver receives an Intent it's listening for (determined by the Intent Filter it uses to register), its

.onReceive( ) method will run (*ON THE MAIN THREAD—yes, capitalized, bolded and italicized)*

In summary

1. sendBroadcast() = the transmitter
2. Intent object = the transmission
3. BroadcastReceiver = the receiver
4. Intent Filter = the frequency your receiver is tuned into
5. onReceive() = the speaker. Sort of.

System events

The Android system generates various events that can be intercepted by Broadcast Receivers. When the system sends these broadcasts, you can set up a receiver to act on them.

The receiver can tune into these events by using an Intent Filter, either in its declaration in the Manifest or when being programmatically created and registered in a Context subclass.

Some of the events that the system generates include

`android.intent.action.BOOT_COMPLETED`

Sent when the system has finished booting. If your app has to take an action as soon as the system boots, you should be listening to this event.

`android.intent.action.BATTERY_LOW`

When the battery is low, this event is broadcast. Maybe you want the device make a farting sound when the battery is low because why not? Not that I ever actually did this.

`android.intent.action.AIRPLANE_MODE`

Sent when you violently throw your phone in the air. Or when the user activates airplane mode. Yeah, definitely one of these. Not sure which one though.

`android.intent.action.WALLPAPER_CHANGED`

Yeah. No explanation needed. Although I'll say that you *could* make your phone make a farting sound when the user changes their wallpaper. Why the hell do you keep mentioning farting, you sicko?

There are many more events that the system can broadcast. Be sure to always check if there's one that can help you accomplish what you want.

Manifest-registered Broadcast Receivers

NOTE: As of Android 8.0 (API level 27) some important restrictions are applied to Manifest-registered broadcast receivers. Read more about it at https://developer.android.com/guide/components/broadcasts under Changes to System Broadcasts.

Remember how you must declare Activity and Service subclasses in the Manifest? You can also do it for Broadcast Receivers using the <receiver /> element. However, *you don't have to.*

In fact, declaring Broadcast Receivers in the Manifest is advised under certain circumstances, while it's not a good idea to do under other circumstances.

A Manifest-registered Broadcast Receiver is always listening for broadcasts, *even when your app is not running.* This can be really useful in some cases.

A Manifest-registered broadcast receiver has to subclass the BroadcastReceiver class and implement its .onReceive() method

```
public class MyBroadcastReceiver extends
BroadcastReceiver {
```

```
@Override
public void onReceive(Context context,
Intent intent) {


Log.i(this.getClass().getSimpleName(), "You
changed your device's wallpaper. What a
guy!");

    }

}
```

This will not simply run when a user changes their wallpaper. You first have to register this Broadcast Receiver subclass in the Manifest, with an Intent Filter that explicitly says to this receiver "Run when you detect that the wallpaper has been changed".

In the same way that you would register an Activity or a Service, you have to add a `<receiver />` element as a child of the the `<application />` element

```
<receiver
android:name=".MyBroadcastReceiver">

            <intent-filter>

            <action
android:name="android.intent.action.WALLPAPER
_CHANGED" />
```

```
        </intent-filter>

    </receiver>
```

You first create a `<receiver >` element and give the `android:name` attribute the BroadcastReceiver's fully-qualified class name.

Then, inside the `<receiver >` element, you create an `<intent-filter >` element as a child and inside the `<intent-filter >` element you create another element called `<action >`

This is where the magic happens: you tell the receiver that it should be activated and its `.onReceive()` method run when an Intent that carries an action of `android.intent.action.WALLPAPER_CHANGED` is broadcast by the system.

So when you change the device's wallpaper, the system sends out a broadcast that says that the wallpaper has been changed and any receivers "interested" (ie. have an Intent Filter tuned into listening to wallpaper changed events) in that broadcast will have their `.onReceive()` methods executed.

Context-registered Broadcast Receivers

Sometimes you want your Broadcast Receiver to only be listening to broadcasts when your application is running in the foreground.

In this case, a Manifest-registered receiver is not appropriate since this type of receiver is constantly listening to broadcasts, even when your app is not running.

To create a Broadcast Receiver that's tied to your Activity's lifecycle, you register it dynamically using Context's `.registerReceiver()` and `.unregisterReceiver()` methods.

Again, we have a receiver

```
public class PimpMyBroadcastReceiver extends
BroadcastReceiver {

@Override
    public void onReceive(Context context, Intent
intent) {


        Log.i(this.getClass().getSimpleName(),
"Your device was just plugged in!");
```

```
        }
}
```

but we don't include any entry about it in the Manifest.

Almost all of the parts are here: you have your transmission (the system sends out a broadcast Intent when the device is plugged in), a receiver and a speaker (the .onReceive() method).

The only thing missing is your receiver tuning into a specific frequency. That is, including an Intent Filter that tunes into the Intent broadcast when the device is plugged in.

Since this Broadcast Receiver does not have an entry in the Manifest, the Intent Filter has to be created programmatically.

```
public class MainActivity extends Activity {

    PimpMyBroadcastReceiver receiver = new
PimpMyBroadcastReceiver();

   @Override
     protected void onCreate(Bundle
savedInstanceState) {
          super.onCreate(savedInstanceState);
          setContentView(R.layout.activity_main);
```

```
}

    @Override
    protected void onResume() {
        IntentFilter filter = new
IntentFilter(Intent.ACTION_POWER_CONNECTED);
        registerReceiver(receiver, filter);
        super.onResume();
    }

    @Override
    protected void onPause() {
        unregisterReceiver(receiver);
        super.onPause();
    }
}
```

These are the interesting lines

```
    PimpMyBroadcastReceiver receiver = new
    PimpMyBroadcastReceiver();
```

Here, we create an instance of our receiver as a class-level variable, so that it will be accessible from within .onPause() and .onResume() - you'll see why in a bit

```
    IntentFilter filter = new
```

```
IntentFilter(Intent.ACTION_POWER_CONNECTED);
```

This is the part where we tune into a frequency. We create an
Intent Filter that will (in a moment) give our receiver the ability
to listen to power-connected events. As mentioned before, there
is a big list of actions that are defined as public static final
Strings in the Intent class and you should always check to see
if there is one available that's relevant to your use case.

```
registerReceiver(receiver, filter);
```

This is the actual registration of the receiver.

The .registerReceiver() method takes two arguments: the
first is the receiver instance we initialized as a member
variable and the second is the Intent Filter we created that
tunes into "power-connected" broadcasts sent by the system.

```
unregisterReceiver(receiver);
```

This is where we unregister the receiver. This has to be done to
avoid a leaked Broadcast Receiver error. Because no-one likes
their broadcast receivers to be leaky, right?

As you have probably noticed, we registered the receiver in
`.onResume()` and unregistered the receiver in `.onPause()`.
This is one possibility. You can also do this

- register the receiver in `.onCreate()` and unregister the
  receiver in `.onDestroy()`
- register the receiver in `.onStart()` and unregister the
  receiver in `.onStop()`

Remember that Context-registered receivers differ from
Manifest-registered receivers in one very important way: they
are only active between the time they have been registered and
the time they have been unregistered.

This means that if MainActivity is not in a resumed state
(visible and with focus), the receiver will not run and no
message will be logged in the logcat when the device is plugged
into power.

`.sendBroadcast()` and your own radio station

Did you think that only the Android system itself is cool enough
to send event broadcasts? Well, think again, you fascist! Thanks
to the tireless efforts of Broadcastists everywhere (and
especially Martin Luther Ping), any Android developer can send
out a broadcast from their app.

To send your own broadcast, simply create an Intent

```
Intent myBroadcastIntent = new
Intent();
```

and supply it with an action String

```
myBroadcastIntent.setAction("com.someth
ing.anApp.someAction");
```

You can also do this in one step by supplying the action String to the Intent constructor like this

```
Intent myBroadcastIntent = new
Intent("com.something.anApp.someAction"
);
```

The action String is the same String value that you pass to the Intent Filter constructor at registration time.

So, if you have created a receiver called AnExampleReceiver and you want its onReceive() method to run whenever an Intent with an action of "com.something.anApp.someAction" is broadcast, this is what you do

```
AnExampleReceiver exampleReceiver = new
AnExampleReceiver();
// in onResume
```

```
IntentFilter filter = new
IntentFilter("com.something.anApp.someA
ction");
registerReceiver(exampleReceiver,
filter)
// don't forget to unregister in
onPause()!!
```

Now that the receiver is registered, when you send a broadcast like this

```
Intent myBroadcastIntent = new
Intent("com.something.anApp.someAction"
);
sendBroadcast(myBroadcastIntent);
```

AnExampleReceiver's .onReceive() method will run, since the action String in the broadcast Intent and the Intent Filter is the same.

The cool part is that onReceive()'s second argument is an Intent object

```
@Override
public void onReceive(Context context,
Intent intent) {
}
```

which is the Intent object that you sent by using the
sendBroadcast() method.

This means that you can use the Intent class's .putExtra()
methods to pass data from an Activity or a Service to a
Broadcast Receiver.

```
Intent myBroadcastIntent = new
Intent("com.something.anApp.someAction"
);

myBroadcastIntent.putExtra("bestShowEve
r", "Firefly");

sendBroadcast(myBroadcastIntent);
```

and retrieve the data in the receiver by going

```
@Override
public void onReceive(Context context,
Intent intent) {
   String show =
intent.getStringExtra("bestShowEver");
// bestShowEver is Firefly. Like, duh
```

```
}
```

Why is this important? Remember in our IntentService chapter, when we downloaded a page from the Internet? Here's the quote

> *But there's still something missing. Wouldn't it be awesome if there was a way to send the downloaded webpage back to the Activity that started the IntentService?*

Well, now you know the way!

Let's go ahead and do that.

Sending data between components

Previously on *Android Development for Gifted Primates*

Dave used the `startService()` *method of Context to start an IntentService from an Activity. The IntentService connected to the internet and started downloading a webpage. While this was happening on a background thread, Sarah was trying to cheat on Alan with Katrina.*

As soon as the webpage was downloaded, the IntentService stopped. This was a huge waste of time, since no-one got any use out of the downloaded webpage. Katrina didn't appreciate Sarah coming on so strong, especially since Alan was her second cousin from her mother's side.

Now Sarah has to figure out a way to keep Katrina's mouth shut. Things are even worse for Dave, who has to find a way to send the downloaded webpage back to the Activity that started the IntentService.

Broadcasting the data from the Intent Service

This is the IntentService code from the previous chapter. I have removed the Notification- related code and replaced the networking-related code with a method that (supposedly) downloads the data to reduce clutter

```java
public class MyIntentService extends IntentService
{

public MyIntentService() {

        super("MyIntentService");

}

@Override

    protected void onHandleIntent(Intent intent) {

    String url = intent.getStringExtra("url");

    String finalPage =
thisMethodGetsThePageFromTheInternet();

    // finalPage is a String that contains the
downloaded page

    // We now have to attach it to an Intent and
send it back to

    // the Activity that started the IntentService

    Intent dataIntent = new Intent();


dataIntent.setAction("com.mycompany.myapp.SEND_DAT
A");

    dataIntent.putExtra("downloadedPage",
finalPage);

    sendBroadcast(dataIntent);
```

```
}

}
```

We create a new Intent and set the Action by using a String of
our choosing (it's good to make sure that this String keeps the
Java package conventions and has a descriptive String about
the action it performs appended at the end, here it's
"SEND_DATA" since we're, uh, sending data)

We then attach the data to our Intent by using the .putExtra()
method and send the broadcast by passing the Intent object to
the sendBroadcast() method.

This is only the first step. We now have to set up a Broadcast
Receiver in the Activity that will receive this Intent.

Receiving the data in the Activity

A very easy way to receive broadcast Intents in our Activity is
to create an anonymous class that implements the
.onReceive() method of Broadcast Receiver. So instead of
doing something like

```
public class MyBroadcastReceiver extends
BroadcastReceiver {
    @Override
```

```
    public void onReceive(Context context,
Intent intent) {
    }
}
```

in a different file, you can do this within the Activity

```
BroadcastReceiver dataReceiver = new
BroadcastReceiver() {
  @Override
    public void onReceive(Context context,
Intent intent) {
    }
}
```

Doing it this way means that the received data will be usable within the Activity.

Here is the complete code for the receiving Activity

```
    public class MainActivity extends Activity {

    BroadcastReceiver rec;

    @Override
```

```java
    protected void onCreate(Bundle
savedInstanceState) {
        super.onCreate(savedInstanceState);

setContentView(R.layout.activity_main);
        rec = new BroadcastReceiver() {
            @Override
            public void onReceive(Context
context, Intent intent) {
                String data =
intent.getStringExtra("downloadedPage");
                Log.i("WEBSITE DATA: ", data);
            }
        };
        IntentFilter filter = new
IntentFilter("com.mycompany.myapp.SEND_DATA")
;
        registerReceiver(rec, filter);
}

    @Override
    protected void onDestroy() {
        unregisterReceiver(rec);
        super.onDestroy();
    }
}
```

Let's go through it

```
BroadcastReceiver rec;
```

Just a simple declaration of a BroadcastReceiver variable. We do not initialize it yet. We need the Broadcast Receiver to be a class-level variable, so we can access it anywhere in MainActivity.

```
rec = new BroadcastReceiver() {
        @Override
        public void onReceive(Context
context, Intent intent) {
            String data =
intent.getStringExtra("downloadedPage")
;
            Log.i("WEBSITE DATA: ",
data);
        }
};
```

Here, we create an implementation of a Broadcast Receiver. Since BroadcastReceiver is an abstract class, we implement onReceive() as usual.

If you remember your Java well, you'll know that this is called an *anonymous class*. Instead of creating a BroadcastReceiver subclass using the extends keyword, we just implement it on the spot.

```
String data =
intent.getStringExtra("downloadedPage")
;
```

Inside the receiver, we extract the String data from the Intent object that's passed to us as the second argument of
.onReceive()

```
Log.i("WEBSITE DATA: ", data);
```

We then log the data, although we could do anything with it, like display it to the user.

```
IntentFilter filter = new
IntentFilter("com.mycompany.myapp.SEND_
DATA");
```

This IntentFilter has the same Action string as the one we gave the Intent object back in the IntentService. Just as a reminder, here's the snippet of the code that sends the broadcast back in the IntentService, with the line where the Action string is set in bold

```
Intent dataIntent = new Intent();
dataIntent.setAction("com.mycompany.mya
pp.SEND_DATA");
dataIntent.putExtra("downloadedPage",
finalPage);
sendBroadcast(dataIntent);
```

Finally, we register the receiver using the registerReceiver() method

```
registerReceiver(rec, filter);
```

We pass the receiver object and the IntentFilter object to the method and sit back and relax. The receiver has been registered with the correct Intent Filter and it's waiting for the IntentService to send the downloaded data back!

Oh, shit! We forgot to unregister the receiver! I think I also left the oven on!

```
@Override
protected void onDestroy() {
    unregisterReceiver(rec);
```

```
        super.onDestroy();
    }
```

Since we registered the receiver in onCreate(), we unregister it in onDestroy().

Remember the lifecycle pairings: **onStart()/onStop()**, **onCreate()/onDestroy()** and **onResume()/onPause()**

And that's it! As soon as the IntentService finishes downloading the webpage and sends the data through the broadcast Intent, the receiver in the Activity will receive the Intent and extract the data from it.

A final note

Dear reader,

You have reached the end of the current edition of the book!

Achievement unlocked, as the kids say these days.

In the first pages of this book, I mentioned that I would avoid covering subjects that I considered unnecessary for beginners, like Content Providers. I also haven't mentioned stuff like Permissions, Fragments, AsyncTasks, Handlers and Loopers.

There is a reason for this: this book is modeled on what I would have liked to know when I was just starting out. Picking up a reference book and trying to learn about OnClickListeners right beside ContentProviders really didn't help me as a beginner.

I will be keeping this book updated with new material, including some of the things I have left out of the first edition of this book. However, such material will be clearly marked as more advanced when those chapters are finally added.

Every buyer of the book will have access to all updated versions, so you can keep learning Android development and new (sometimes made-up!) swear words at the same time.

I really want to thank you for purchasing this book and encourage you to send me an e-mail at sebastian212000@gmail.com if you have any questions, suggestions or simply
want to chat!

Talk to you soon,

Antonis.

PS. If you liked the book, please remember to leave a review on the book's Amazon page at https://www.amazon.com/Android-Development-Gifted-Primates-Beginners-ebook/dp/B07FYSKVYY if you can spare a minute or two! It would *really* mean a lot to me. Thanks!

Made in the USA
Middletown, DE
01 July 2020

11652198R00144